# MATTHEW
# VIRGINAL CONCEPTION

*In Light of Palestinian and Hellenistic
Judaic Traditions on the Birth of
Israel's First Redeemer, Moses*

## Roger David Aus

## Studies in Judaism

University Press of America,® Inc.
Lanham · Boulder · New York · Toronto · Oxford

**Copyright © 2004 by**
**University Press of America,® Inc.**
4501 Forbes Boulevard
Suite 200
Lanham, Maryland 20706
UPA Acquisitions Department (301) 459-3366

PO Box 317
Oxford
OX2 9RU, UK

Library of Congress Control Number: 2004112250
ISBN 0-7618-3038-3 (paperback : alk. ppr.)

# Studies in Judaism

# Dedicated

## to

all those who at least *try* to understand the nature of, and to
appreciate, Judaic and early Jewish Christian haggadah

# Table of Contents

# Preface

Every Sunday millions of Christians in hundreds of different languages confess throughout the world that Jesus Christ "was conceived by the power of the Holy Spirit and born of the virgin Mary" (Apostles' Creed), or that "by the power of the Holy Spirit he became incarnate from the virgin Mary, and was made man" (Nicene Creed). Mary's fiancé and later husband, Joseph, appears to have been intentionally omitted in order to emphasize the miraculous aspect of Jesus' birth: while biologically impossible according to human standards, the prophet from Nazareth was born of Mary, who conceived him as a virgin. The latter is maintained in the only two birth narratives found in the Gospels: Luke 1:34-35 and Matt 1:18, 20, 23 and 25.

The following study deals almost exclusively with the Matthean birth narrative, although I also occasionally call attention in the notes to aspects of the Lukan account. The main reason for this is that the Matthean birth narrative, as has long been recognized, is in part dependent on early Judaic sources which comment on the birth of Israel's future redeemer Moses in Exodus 1-2. I list these sources in the Introduction and then proceed to analyze Matthew's use of phraseology and motifs from them.

It is within the Judaic complex of the miraculous birth of Moses that the motif of "virginity" is already greatly emphasized, primarily in regard to his very aged mother Jochebed, but also in regard to his sister Miriam (Latin Maria, English Mary). I shall attempt to show how a combination of Palestinian and Hellenistic Judaic comment on Jochebed and Miriam within the context of Moses' birth led to Matthew's appropriation from his own Jewish Christian community of the Holy Spirit's "coming upon" Miriam, and of a "virgin's" conceiving one who would redeem his people.

In section VIII. at the end of this study I briefly deal with the question of the historicity of Mary's virginal conception, including the nature of Judaic "haggadah" (see pp. 2 and 80 on this), unfortunately unknown to most contemporary Christians. My own Christian faith (and I am a Lutheran pastor) is not dependent on a personal or ecclesiastical affirmation of the virginal conception, but on the Crucifixion and Resurrection of Jesus. In spite of my disagreeing with much further development of Marian veneration, especially the later Roman Catholic dogmas proclaimed in connection with it, this study should not be viewed as "anti-" Roman Catholic. As I point out in the Ecumenical Epilogue, many Protestants today can rightly rediscover positive aspects of Mary's portrayal in the "New" Testament after centuries of neglecting her.

One result of the following study is my demonstrating how the Evangelist Matthew, himself a bilingual Jewish Christian, in his own birth narrative was heavily dependent on both early Palestinian and Hellenistic Judaic traditions on the birth of Moses. In this regard the investigation appropriately fits Professor Jacob Neusner's series "Studies in Judaism," and I cordially thank him for generously accepting it here.

My thanks also go to Maurice Casey of the University of Nottingham, England, Tal Ilan, Niko Oswald and Irina Wandrey of the Free University of Berlin's Institut für Judaistik, and Peter von der Osten-Sacken of the Humboldt University's Institut Kirche und Judentum, who critically read the manuscript. David Bartlett of Yale University, Richard Kalmin of The Jewish Theological Seminary of America in New York City, and David Instone-Brewer of Cambridge, England, kindly obtained several pieces of literature which were not available to me in Berlin. The Rev. Dr. Thomas Day graciously proofread it, and my son Jonathan Aus generously took time off from his own doctoral work in Oslo to type part of the study and to format all of it.

My emphasis in this investigation has been on letting the primary sources speak for themselves, a number of which are not easily accessible. Wherever possible I have cited the earliest available form of a tradition. The very few patently late sources I note, such as Sefer ha-Yashar and the Zohar, should only be seen as *possibly* containing remnants of such earlier traditions. When not offering my own translations of rabbinic sources, I cite the standard English and Hebrew / Aramaic editions in abbreviated form. They are described more fully in "Sources and Reference Works" at the end of the volume. Since the secondary literature on Matthew 1-2 and the virginal conception is extremely large, I have only attempted to dialogue with the major positions found there as that literature has been available to me in Berlin, not wanting to overburden the footnotes. An index of modern authors is included, especially in order to indicate where I differ from modern interpreters.

It is my hope that this investigation may aid in recovering a clearer picture of Mary, the very young Jewish mother of Jesus, whose name, as noted above, millions of Christians mention every Sunday in the confession of their faith. May it also aid contemporary Jews in appreciating how much the earliest Jewish Christians borrowed from Judaic traditions on the birth of Moses in order to describe the circumstances of the birth of Jesus.

Roger David Aus
Pentecost, 2004
Berlin, Germany

# Introduction

It has long been recognized that the birth story of Jesus in Matt 1:18–2:23 is influenced by the birth story of Moses in Exodus 1-2, especially as reflected in Judaic tradition.[1] One major reason for this is the standard dictum: "As the first redeemer (Moses) was, so the last (or great) redeemer (the Messiah) will be."[2] An example of this with the messianic king is found in the Moses infancy narrative in *Exod. Rab.* Shemoth 1/26 on Exod 2:10.[3] While not wishing to follow in well-trodden

---

[1] Cf. Str-B *ad loc.*; Paul Winter, "Jewish Folklore in the Matthean Birth Story" in *Hibbert Journal* 53 (1954-55) 34-42; Charles Perrot, "Les récits d'enfance dans la Haggada antérieure au IIᵉ siècle de notre ère" in *RSR* 55 (1967) 481-518, especially 497-504; Samuel Lachs, *A Rabbinic Commentary on the New Testament. The Gospels of Matthew, Mark and Luke* (Hoboken, NJ: KTAV Publishing House, 1987) 5-14; Allan Kensky, "Moses and Jesus: The Birth of the Savior," in *Judaism* 42 (1993) 43-49; Jonathan Cohen, *The Origins and Evolution of the Moses Nativity Story* (Studies in the History of Religions 58; Leiden: Brill, 1993), esp. 157-171, although he concentrates here on Matt 2:1-12; Arland Hultgren, "Matthew's Infancy Narrative and the Nativity of an Emerging Community" in *Horizons in Biblical Theology* 19 (1997) 91-108; Raymond Brown, *The Birth of the Messiah. A Commentary on the Infancy Narratives in Matthew and Luke* (Garden City, NY: Doubleday, 1993²); the commentaries on Matthew, especially those of W. D. Davies and Dale C. Allison, Jr., *The Gospel According to Saint Matthew* (Edinburgh: T. and T. Clark, 1988) 1.190-195 on "The Sources of Mt 1.18-23," and 196-284, and Ulrich Luz, *Das Evangelium nach Matthäus* (EKK I/1; Düsseldorf and Zurich: Benziger; Neukirchen-Vluyn: Neukirchener, 2002⁵) 1.140-199; and Dale C. Allison, Jr., *The New Moses. A Matthean Typology* (Minneapolis: Augsburg Fortress, 1993) 140-165. The latter work became available to me only after I finished this study. However, where relevant I will refer to it in the footnotes. In my *Weihnachten, Barmherziger Samariter, Verlorener Sohn. Studien zu ihrem jüdischen Hintergrund* (ANTZ 2; Berlin: Institut Kirche und Judentum, 1988) 11-58, I also call attention to Judaic haggadic traditions on the infancy narrative of Moses as the major background of Luke 2:1-20.

[2] Cf. the many examples in Str-B 1.68-70, as well as 85-88 on the redemption from Egypt as prefiguring the messianic redemption.

[3] Mirqin 5.41, Soncino 3.33. A parallel is found in *Tanḥ.* Shemoth 8 on Exod 2:6 (Eshkol 1.213, Berman 325).

paths, in the following study I will by necessity also call attention to several motifs and expressions already noted by others. However, I will illuminate them from Judaic, especially rabbinic sources which I interpret in new ways. My argument culminates in the assertion that a major part of the virginal conception of Jesus by Mary derives from Palestinian Judaic haggadic[4] embellishment of the Moses infancy narrative. It was then supplemented by Hellenistic Jewish concern with virginal conception by the matriarchs and other female Israelite heroes.

Moses' birth narrative was very popular in Judaic tradition, from the time of the  Septuagint to the later midrashim. The following examples show this.[5]

---

[4] On haggadah, cf. section VIII. below. Here it suffices to note that it includes the imaginative filling-in of gaps assumed to be in a text, thus it is an expansion of them.

[5] For an almost encyclopedic coverage of them, cf. Louis Ginzberg, *The Legends of the Jews* 2.245-276 and the notes in 5.391-404. See also the articles "Amram, Father of Moses," "In Rabbinical Literature," by Kaufmann Kohler in *EJ* (1901) 1.533-534; "Amram" in *JE* (1971) 2.890; "Jochebed" by M. Seligsohn in *EJ* (1904) 7.203; "Jochebed" in *JE* (1971) 10.130; "Miriam" by Jacob Lauterbach in *EJ* (1904) 8.608-609, and by Aaron Rothkoff in *JE* (1971) 12.82-84; and "Moses" by Jacob Lauterbach in *EJ* (1905) 9.46-49, and Aaron Rothkoff in *JE* (1971) 12.395-398. See also Renée Bloch, *Moïse, l'Homme de l'Alliance* (Tournai: Desclée & Cie., 1955), available to me as *Moses in Schrift und Überlieferung*, ed. F. Stier and E. Beck (Düsseldorf: Patmos-Verlag, 1963). In addition, the Samaritan account of the birth of Moses, the *Molad Mosheh*, explicitly cites Exod 2:1-10 and comments on the passage extensively. While it patently borrows from the Christian nativity accounts of Jesus (e.g. the star of Moses, the angelic choir at his birth), it has also preserved much Judaic haggadic material. See Selig J. Miller, *Molad Mosheh*, which contains two Arabic MSS and a Samaritan Aramaic MS, with English translations. The *Asatir*, in Samaritan Aramaic with an Arabic commentary, the Pitron, also describes the birth of Moses in 8:24−9:14. See Moses Gaster, *The Asatir* 270-278 for an English translation, and 36-39 at the end of the volume for the Aramaic. The respective introductions by Miller and Gaster discuss the problems involved in dating the materials, yet Gaster's view of the middle or end of the third century BCE for the *Asatir* (Preface and 160) is untenable. Both documents in their present form are medieval.

## 1. The Septuagint

From the third century BCE,[6] the LXX already shows the influence of haggadic tradition. Exod 1:5 for example has the number 75 instead of 70 in the Hebrew; 1:11 adds "On, which is Heliopolis"; 1:22 adds "to the Hebrews"; and 2:2b-3a changes the subject of the verbs from "she" to "they."

## 2. Ezekiel the Tragedian

Written in Greek and perhaps from Alexandria during the first part of the second century BCE,[7] Ezekiel the Tragedian's work "The Exodus" in lines 1-31 reveals haggadic embellishments of the biblical account. Examples are Jochebed's first "robing" the infant Moses before exposing him in the marsh near the river (line 16 on Exod 2:3) and the fourfold emphasis on "straightway," "running," "quickly" and "with haste" in lines 21-26.[8]

## 3. Jubilees

Written in Hebrew in Palestine probably around 150 BCE,[9] Jubilees in 46:11 − 47:12 retells Exod 1:1 − 2:14. Concerned with the exact chronology of the narrated events, this writing also betrays very early haggadic amplifications such as the statement in 47:4, "And your mother came in the night and suckled you and (in) the day Miriam, your sister, guarded you from the birds." In v 5 it notes that the name of Pharaoh' s daughter was "Tharmuth," and in v 9 that Moses' father Amram taught him writing.[10]

---

[6] Cf. Otto Eissfeldt, *The Old Testament. An Introduction* (Oxford: Basil Blackwell, 1966) 604-605, 702-703.

[7] Cf. the remarks of R. G. Robertson in *OTP* 2.803-804.

[8] *OTP* 2.808-809. For the relevance of the latter motif to Miriam as an ʿalmah, cf. section V. below.

[9] Cf. O. S. Wintermute in *OTP* 2.43-45.

[10] *OTP* 2.138.

## 4. Philo

This Alexandrian philosopher, who perhaps died ca. 50 CE,[11] wrote many treatises in Greek, including "De Vita Mosis." In 1.5-18 he retells Exodus 1-2, incorporating haggadic traditions he has learned from others.[12] Examples are his assertion that Amram and Jochebed were "the best of their contemporaries," and Moses was the seventh in descent from Abraham (7); his parents exposed him "with tears" at the river and departed "groaning" (10), reproaching themselves for not casting him away already at his birth (11); the king's daughter had no sisters and "had been married for a considerable time but had not conceived a child" (13); and she called the child Moses, "for the Egyptians call water *mou*" (17).

## 5. Pseudo-Philo

Originally written in Hebrew in Palestine, probably in the first half of the first century CE,[13] Pseudo-Philo retells Exodus 1-2 with many haggadic additions in his chapter 9. It has Amram for example hold a long monologue (3-6) before the elders of the people in regard to whether they should refrain from having intercourse with their wives in order to avoid the results of Exod 1:22. In 10 the writer notes that "the spirit of God came upon Miriam," and that God will save His people through the son to be born to her parents, as revealed to Miriam by an

---

[11] Cf. Erwin Goodenough, *An Introduction to Philo Judaeus* (Oxford: Basil Blackwell, 1962²) 2.

[12] Cf. φασί, "we are told," in 9 and 13. In 4 he notes that he tells the Moses story as he has learned it on the basis of the sacred books (the Bible), and from some of the elders of the nation. He interweaves what he has read with what he has been told. On him see also Louis Feldman, "Philo's View of Moses' Birth and Upbringing" in *CBQ* 64 (2002) 258-281.

[13] Cf. Daniel Harrington in *OTP* 2.298-300.

angel in a dream. In addition, Pharaoh's daughter called Moses "Melchiel" (16).[14]

## 6. Josephus

A native of Jerusalem of priestly descent, whose native tongue was Aramaic, Josephus was born in 37-38 CE and completed his *Jewish Antiquities* in 93-94 CE.[15] In *Ant.* 2.201-237 (ix.1-7) he retells Exodus 1-2 with many Palestinian haggadic embellishments. Three examples are the name of the Egyptian king's daughter, Thermouthis (224); Moses as seventh in descent from Abraham (229); and the infant's taking the king's diadem from his own head, unto which it had been placed, flinging it to the ground, and trampling it underfoot. Therefore an advisor says he should be killed (233-236). If the latter legend were not found in Josephus, one would probably attribute its occurrence in rabbinic sources[16] to a much later time. This is an example of how material now found in much later rabbinic works can actually be attested for the first century CE. Each such instance must be examined by itself.

## 7. The Midrashim

A running haggadic commentary on Exod 1:1 – 2:10 is found in *Exodus Rabbah* Shemoth 1/1-26,[17] and for much of the same biblical narrative in *b. Soṭah* 11a-13a.[18] Other rabbinic works also contain comment on some of these verses, and I will cite them when they are appropriate. The following Tannaim, the earliest

---

14 *OTP* 2.315-316. In 316, n. "k," Harrington calls attention to "striking parallels between Moses' birth as narrated here and that of Jesus in Mt 1f...."

15 Cf. his *Bell.* 1.3; *Vita* 1, 5; and *Ant.* 20.267. On him see also Louis Feldman, "Josephus' Portrait of Moses" in *JQR* 82 (1992) 285-328, esp. 293-303.

16 Cf. *Exod. Rab.* Shemoth 1/26 on Exod 2:10 and the *Tanḥuma* parallel cited in n. 3. For another such example from Josephus, see n. 76 in section V.

17 Mirqin 5.9-42, Soncino 3.1-34.

18 Soncino 52-65.

known rabbinic authorities, expound the above scriptural material, and I cite them primarily from the works noted above.

1. R. Ishmael (b. Elisha), a second generation Tanna,[19] in *Midr. Prov.* 22:20 with Exod 2:2.[20]
2. R. Akiba, a second generation Tanna,[21] in *Exod. Rab.* Shemoth 1/12.[22]
3. R. Yoshiyyah, a third generation Tanna,[23] in *Exod. Rab.* Shemoth 1/20 on Exod 2:2.[24]
4. R. Meir, a third generation Tanna,[25] in *Exod. Rab.* Shemoth 1/20 on Exod 2:2,[26] *Tanḥ.* B Shemoth 8 on Exod 1:9,[27] and *b. Soṭah* 12a on Exod 2:2.[28]
5. R. Simeon b. Yoḥai, a third generation Tanna,[29] in *b. Soṭah* 12b on Exod 2:5.[30]
6. R. Judah (b. Ilai), a third generation Tanna,[31] in *Exod. Rab.* Shemoth 1/20 on Exod 2:2, 1/23 on Exod 2:5, 1/24 on Exod 2:6,[32] and *b. Soṭah* 12a on Exod 2:2, and 12b on Exod 2:5 and 6.[33]
7. R. Nehemiah, a third generation Tanna,[34] in *Exod. Rab.* Shemoth 1/23 on Exod 2:5, and 1/24 on Exod 2:6,[35] and *b. Soṭah* 12a on Exod 2:2, and 12b on Exod 2:5 and 2:6.[36]

---

[19] Cf. H. Strack and G. Stemberger, *Introduction to the Talmud and Midrash* 79.
[20] Buber 92, Visotzky 98.
[21] *Introduction* 79.
[22] Mirqin 5.23, Soncino 3.15.
[23] *Introduction* 83.
[24] Mirqin 5.34, Soncino 3.26.
[25] *Introduction* 84.
[26] Mirqin 5.34, Soncino 3.26.
[27] Buber 2.5, Townsend 7.
[28] Soncino 61.
[29] *Introduction* 84.
[30] Soncino 62.
[31] *Introduction* 84.
[32] Cf. respectively Mirqin 5.33-34, 37, 38; Soncino 3.26, 29 and 30.
[33] Cf. respectively Soncino 61 and 62.
[34] *Introduction* 85.
[35] Cf. respectively Mirqin 5.37 and 38; Soncino 3.29 and 30.

8. The School of R. Eleazar b. R. Simeon (b. Yoḥai), a fourth generation Tanna,[37] in *Exod. Rab.* Shemoth 1/10 on Exod 1:11,[38] and *b. Soṭah* 11a also on the latter verse.[39]

9. R. Ḥiyya b. Abba, a fifth generation Tanna,[40] in *b. Soṭah* 11a on Exod 1:10.[41]

10. R. Simai, a fifth generation Tanna,[42] in *b. Soṭah* 11a on Exod 1:10.[43]

11. In addition, Tannaitic tradition is given as "It is taught" ( תַּנְיָא ) in *Exod. Rab.* Shemoth 1/21 on Exod 2:3, 1/23 on Exod 2:5, and 1/25 on Exod 2:7,[44] as well as in *b. Soṭah* 11a on Exod 1:9, 11b on Exod 1:15, 11b on Exod 1:17b, 12a on Exod 2:1, 12a on Exod 2:3, and 12b on Exod 2:6. [45]

In light of the very early haggadic embellishment of Exodus 1-2 pointed out in the other Judaic sources adduced in sections 1.–6. above, there is no justification for doubting that the statements made by the Tannaim cited above most probably derive from them. It also raises the *possibility* that some of the traditions now found in anonymous form in later rabbinic works could also be very early, as the example I cited at the end of 6. shows.

As remarked above, in the following study I will point out how Palestinian haggadic embellishment of Moses' birth narrative found in Exodus 1-2 provides a major part of the virginal conception of Jesus by Mary within the birth narrative of Matthew 1-2. Before doing so, however, several remarks will

---

[36] Cf. Soncino 61 and 62.
[37] *Introduction* 87.
[38] Mirqin 5.20, Soncino 3.12.
[39] Soncino 54.
[40] *Introduction* 90.
[41] Soncino 53.
[42] *Introduction* 91.
[43] Soncino 53-54.
[44] Cf. respectively Mirqin 5.35, 37 and 39, and Soncino 3.27, 29 and 32.
[45] Cf. respectively Soncino 53, 57, 58, 60 and 62 (twice).

be helpful in regard to the development of the christological statement that Jesus is the "Son of God."[46]

The earliest NT texts speak of Jesus' becoming the Son of God at his Resurrection. Rom 1:4, for example, states that God's Son, descended from David according to the flesh, "was declared to be Son of God with power according to the Holy Spirit by resurrection from the dead."[47] The earliest Gospel, that of Mark, from shortly before or after 70 CE, places this declaration already at Jesus' baptism. There a voice from heaven tells him, when the Spirit descends upon him like a dove: "You are My Son, the Beloved; with you I am well pleased" (1:11).[48] The first part of this is then repeated at the Transfiguration (9:7).

The other two Synoptic Gospels, later and in part dependent on Mark, trace the recognition of Jesus as God's Son to a yet earlier period. In Luke 2:41-52, for example, the Evangelist describes the twelve-year-old Jesus in the Jerusalem Temple. When Mary informs him that his father (Joseph) and she had been searching for him with great  anxiety, he asks her why. "Did you not know that I must be in my Father's house?" (v 49). In other words, Jesus is God's "Son." Elsewhere I have pointed out that the Palestinian Jewish Christian  who first composed this narrative, later appropriated by Luke in Greek, applied Judaic haggadic traditions on the twelve-year-old Samuel to Jesus. There the youth is represented as pilgrimaging to the

---

[46] Cf. the sections on the "Son of God" in the still valid volumes of Oscar Cullmann, *The Christology of the New Testament* (Philadelphia: Westminster, 1963) 270-305, and Reginald Fuller, *The Foundations of New Testament Christology* (New York: Charles Scribner's Sons, 1965) 31-33, 65, 114-115, 164-167, 187-188, 192-197, and 231-232, especially 195-196.

[47] Cf. Acts 13:33, quoting Ps 2:7.

[48] The statement brings Ps 2:7 and Isa 42:1 together. For this combination, cf. *Midr. Pss.* 2/9 on Ps 2:7 (Buber 28, Braude 1.40-41). After Ps 110:1 and Dan 7:13-14 are cited, the assertion is made that all of these promises will be fulfilled in the messianic king. Anti-Christian polemic follows.  For Ps 2:7 and the Messiah, see also *b. Sukk.* 52a (Soncino 247) and *Cant. Zuṭa* 1:1 (Buber 2).

temple in Shiloh with his parents and like a child prodigy instructing the priests there how to sacrifice properly.[49]

Just as Palestinian Judaic haggadic traditions on the young Israelite folk hero Samuel were applied to the twelve-year-old Jesus, so Palestinian haggadic embellishment of the birth of the greatest Israelite of all, Moses, was applied by the bilingual Jewish Christian Matthew[50] to Jesus, now however already at his birth. Within a narrative saturated with motifs and expressions from the Moses birth haggadah (1:18−25), Matthew himself adds a citation of LXX Isa 7:14. Here a virgin (Mary is meant prophetically by Matthew) will bear a son, whose name will be "God is with us" (v 23). In other words, the son of the virgin is also the Son of God. This is corroborated in 2:15, where within Herod's search for the newborn king of the Jews (reminiscent of Pharaoh's search for the newborn Moses in order to kill him), the Evangelist quotes Hos 11:1 to mean: "Out of Egypt I have called My Son." Here too the infant Jesus is described indirectly as the Son of God.

The longer early Christians pondered over Jesus' relation to the Father, the further his Sonship was taken back: from the Resurrection to the baptism, to him at the age of twelve, and finally to his birth.[51] They argued that if Jesus was God's Son at the Resurrection, he certainly must already have been so when

---

[49] Cf. my study "The Child Jesus in the Temple (Luke 2:41-51a), and Judaic Traditions on the Child Samuel in the Temple (1 Samuel 1-3)" in *Samuel, Saul and Jesus. Three Early Palestinian Jewish Christian Gospel Haggadoth* (SFSHJ 105; Atlanta: Scholars Press, 1994) 1-64.

[50] Cf. for example W. D. Davies and Dale Allison, Jr., *The Gospel According to Saint Matthew* 1.26, 80, 262 and 267, as well as my studies "The Magi at the Birth of Cyrus, and the Magi at Jesus' Birth in Matt 2:1-12" in *New Perspectives on Ancient Judaism* 2, ed. Jacob Neusner et al. (Howard C. Kee Festschrift; Lanham, MD: University Press of America, 1987) 99-114; Peter's sinking in the Sea of Galilee in Matt 14:28-31 in *"Caught in the Act," Walking on the Sea, and the Release of Barabbas Revisited* (SFSHJ 157; Atlanta: Scholars Press, 1998) 98-110; and "An Earthquake and Saints Rising from the Dead" (Matt 27:51b-53) in *Samuel, Saul and Jesus* 116-133.

[51] The Evangelist John carries this back still further. As the Word, Jesus was already with God at the beginning (of the world): 1:1-2.

he was born. It is in the context of this relatively "late" christology that the virginal conception of Jesus must be seen. Its main original purpose was to express in the form of a narrative, based in part on God's miraculously restoring the youth and virginity of Jochebed so that she could bear the first redeemer of Israel (see below), that Jesus, the final redeemer of Israel, in a miraculous way was the Son of God already at his birth. His biological father was thus described as not being Joseph, but God.[52]

The following study has eight sections: I. Flight to Egypt Because of Mortal Danger, and Return from there at the Death of the Persecutor;  II. Astrologers' Announcement to the King of the Birth of Israel's Savior, and the King's Dread;  III. Searching for the Newborn Child in Order to Destroy It, Up to the Age of Two, and Jer 31:15;  IV. Mary, Miriam and the Holy Spirit, and the Infants Jesus and Moses as Future Saviors;  V. The Marriages of Joseph and Mary, and Amram and Jochebed;  VI. Other Parallels to the Virginal Conception from the History of

---

[52] In light of the results reached below, it is unnecessary to consider here the details of the modern thesis that Mary was raped, making Jesus illegitimate. The virginal conception was thus ostensibly a cover-up for this phenomenon. Cf. Jane Schaberg, *The Illegitimacy of Jesus* (San Francisco: Harper & Row, 1987); Gerd Lüdemann, *Virgin Birth? The Real Story of Mary and Her Son Jesus* (Harrisburg, PA: Trinity Press International, 1998) 78 and 138; and Marianne Sawicki, *Crossing Galilee. Architectures of Contact in the Occupied Land of Jesus* (Harrisburg, PA: Trinity Press International, 2000) 192-193. In his study *The Historical Mary. Revealing the Pagan Identity of the Virgin Mother* (Berkeley, CA: Seastone, 2003), the journalist Michael Jordan attributes great historical value to later sources from the NT Apocrypha and Gnosticism. Borrowing the motif of Mary's being brought up in the Jerusalem Temple as of the age of three from the Protevangelium of James 7:2, for example, Jordan maintains that instead of the aged and "probably impotent" Joseph, "more realistically, Mary's partner in the Sacred Marriage was a temple High Priest who acted as proxy to the king." For this reason Jesus during his lifetime "more or less distanced himself from her..." (p. 297). Jordan also contends that "we have found evidence for the existence of an apocryphal work, the *Genna Marias*, indicating that Jesus committed incest, on at least one occasion, with his mother" (p. 298).

Religions; VII. Jewish Allegations of Jesus' Illegitimacy; and VIII. Haggadah and the Historicity of the Virginal Conception. "An Ecumenical Epilogue" concludes the investigation.

# I. Flight to Egypt Because of Mortal Danger, and Return from there at the Death of the Persecutor

A clear indication that Matthew had the early history of Moses in mind when he formulated his infancy narrative in 1:18-2:23 is found almost at the end of this section. In 2:13-15 an angel of the Lord appears to Joseph in a dream and tells him to flee with Jesus and Mary to Egypt and to remain there until he informs them (to return), for Herod is about to search for the child in order to destroy it. Joseph thereupon obediently follows these instructions, staying there (in Egypt) until the death of Herod.

The Evangelist Matthew at this point inserts the third of four formula quotations[53] in the infancy narrative in 2:15 : "Out of Egypt I have called My Son" (Hos 11:1b). Here God's "son" is meant as Jesus, as at his baptism in Matt 3:17. Originally, however, it was meant as Israel, as specifically stated in Hos 11:1a.

The latter passage is cited by Abraham Saba, a Spanish exegete who died ca. 1508 CE, in his commentary on the Pentateuch, *Ṣeror ha-Mor*, in regard to Exod 2:6. The connection is via the catchword "youth" ( נַעַר ) in both biblical verses. Saba here quotes from an undatable "midrash" which has unfortunately not come down to us. If it contained some remnants of very early material, at least in this particular instance, the Judaic application of Hos 11:1 to Moses in his birth narrative *may* have been known to Matthew, causing him to quote the same verse at 2:15.

The same "midrash" then applies Jer 31:9 to the boy Moses' "weeping" in Exod 2:6.[54] As will be shown in section III. 4.

---

[53] The others are the fulfillment quotations in 1:22-23 and 2:17-18, as well as what is written by the prophet (Micah) in 2:5-6. For a fulfillment quotation in connection with Exod 2:1, see *Mek. R. Šim. b. Yoḥ.* ( Epstein / Melamed 6 ): לקיים מה שנאמר.

[54] Cf. Menahem M. Kasher's *Encyclopedia of Biblical Interpretation* 7.44-45; the Hebrew is found in his *Torah Shelemah* 8.66 on section 51, as well as the full text in *Ṣeror ha-Mor*, ed. Jacob Meir Weichleder (Benei Barak: Hechal ha-Sepher, 1990) 1.348-349, with n. 30. See the art. "Saba,

below, the Zohar applies Jer 31:15 also to Exod 2:6, and Matthew quotes Jer 31:15 at 2:18. Various verses from Jeremiah 31, including 3 and 20, were also connected to Moses' birth by the Zohar and earlier sources. It is thus possible that Hos 11:1 and Jeremiah 31, both connected to Moses' birth narrative by the otherwise unknown "midrash" Abraham Saba quotes on Exod 2:6, *may* have been connected also at a much earlier time, causing Matthew to employ both of them in the birth narrative of Israel's final redeemer, the Messiah Jesus, only three verses apart (2:15 and 18).

Steeped in the Bible, Matthew knew very well that Israel as the Lord's son in Hos 11:1 was already emphasized in Exod 4:22-23.[55] This aided him in borrowing imagery from the nearby verse 19 and applying it at the end of his own narrative.

After the "massacre of the infants" in Matt 2:16-18, the danger for the child Jesus passed with the death of Herod in v 19. At this point Matthew reverses the procedure of verses 13-15. The same angel of the Lord now appears in a dream to Joseph in Egypt and instructs him in v 20: "Get up, take the child and his mother, and go to the land of Israel, *for those who were seeking the child's life are dead.*" This Joseph obediently carries out in v 21.

The italicized imagery of v 20 derives from Exod 4:19, where the Lord tells Moses: "Go back to Egypt; *for all those who were seeking your life are dead.*" Thus Joseph, like Moses,[56] takes his wife and son and returns to the land from which they had fled, Palestine. It is of course true that Moses flees with his family *from* a danger in Egypt and later returns there, whereas Joseph with his family flees from a danger in Palestine *to* Egypt and later returns to Palestine. The main points of connection for

---

Abraham ben Jacob" by Shmuel Ashkenazi in *EJ* (1971) 14.555-556 on his commentary and dates.

[55] Cf. Douglas Stuart, *Hosea-Jonah* (WBC 31; Waco, TX: Word Books, 1987) 177: "Yahweh's words in Hos 11:1 are best understood in light of Exod 4:22-23..." and 178 on Matt 2:15, as well as Francis Andersen and David Noel Freedman, *Hosea* (AB 24; Garden City, NY: Doubleday, 1980) 577.

[56] It should be noted that Moses' flight to Midian in the unit Exod 2:11-15 takes place directly after the end of his birth narrative in 2:10.

Matthew, however, were the catchword "Egypt"; flight from a mortal danger; and return from the land of exile once the danger from the persecutor(s) had passed (for Joseph at the death of Herod in 4 BCE). In order to describe this, the Evangelist intentionally borrowed imagery from the early life of Moses in Exodus 4. Most of his other allusions and motifs he then appropriated from the narrative of Moses' infancy preceding this in chapters 1-2, especially as elaborated in Judaic tradition.

## II. Astrologers' Announcement to the King of the Birth of Israel's Savior, and the King's Dread

After Jesus was born in Bethlehem, wise men or astrologers ( μάγοι )[57] from the East went to Jerusalem and asked: " Where is the child who has been born king of the Jews? For we observed his star at its rising, and have come to pay him homage" (Matt 2:2). "When King Herod heard this, 'he was frightened' (ἐταράχθη),[58] and all Jerusalem with him" (v 3). Therefore he called together all the chief priests and scribes of the people and inquired of them where the Messiah was to be born. They answered: in Bethlehem of Judea (vv 5-6).

The above imagery of astrologers who note the birth of the new king,[59] leading to the reigning king's becoming greatly frightened, derives from Judaic comment on Pharaoh and the birth of Moses.

Like Herod, Pharaoh is also labelled "the king" (of Egypt) in Exod 1:15, 17 and 18 (cf. also 8). Josephus in *Ant.* 2.205 notes that "One of the sacred scribes ( ἱερογραμματέων )[60] – persons with considerable skill in accurately predicting the future – announced to the king that there would be born to the Israelites at that time one who would abase the sovereignty of the Egyptians and exalt the Israelites, were he reared to manhood...." Moses is of course meant.

By "sacred scribes" Josephus most probably has in mind here the "magicians" of Egypt, called a חַרְטֹם in Gen 41:8 and 24 and elsewhere. Derived from חֶרֶט , a stylus,[61] the term engraver, writer was only employed of "one possessed of occult knowledge, *diviner, astrologer, magician*."[62] It is precisely these

---

[57] BAGD 484-485 on μάγος.
[58] BAGD 805 on ταράσσω : pass. be troubled, frightened, terrified.
[59] In Palestinian Judaic sources the Messiah was always thought of as a king, as in the standard expression מֶלֶךְ הַמָּשִׁיחַ , "the king, the Messiah" or "the messianic king." Cf. Str-B 1.6-7.
[60] Cf. also 209 and 234. The sacred scribes, pl., of the Egyptians are also noted in 243.
[61] BDB 354-355.
[62] BDB 355.

Egyptian astrologers whom Symmachus translates with μάγοι
in the above two Genesis passages. There were also חַרְטֻמִּים in
Babylonia (Dan 1:20, 2:2), making the magi "from the East" in
Matt 2:1 appropriate.[63]
Josephus speaks of "one" of the sacred scribes as announcing
to king Pharaoh the birth of Israel's liberator. In rabbinic
tradition there are instead three advisors to Pharaoh who do so.
They include Balaam,[64] who predicted in Num 24:17 that "a star
shall come out of Jacob, and a sceptre shall rise out of Israel."
This passage was interpreted messianically in Judaic sources,[65]
and it forms part of the background of the star of the newborn
messianic king in Matthew 2.

Rabbinic sources speak of Pharaoh's advisors as
"astrologers."[66] In *b. Sanh.* 101b, for example, "Our Rabbis
taught" that "three beheld but did not see," including Pharaoh's
"astrologers"( אִיצטגנינּי ).[67] R. Ḥama b. Ḥanina, a second
generation Palestinian Amora,[68] then asks what the phrase "This
is the water of Meribah" (Num 20:13) means. He maintains:
"'This is' what Pharaoh's astrologers saw, but erred [in its
interpretation]. They saw that Israel's saviour ( מושׁיע ) would
be smitten through water. Therefore he [Pharaoh] ordered
'Every son that is born you shall cast into the River [Nile]'
(Exod 1:22). Yet they did not know that he was to be smitten

---

63 Cf. also *Eccl. Rab.* 7:23 § 1 (Soncino 8.203) regarding the wisdom of
"the children of the east" (1 Kgs 5:10) : "They were skilled in
astrology...."
64 Cf. Judith Baskin, *Pharaoh's Counsellors. Job, Jethro and Balaam in
Rabbinic and Patristic Tradition* (BJS 47: Chico, CA: Scholars Press,
1983) 75-113 on Balaam.
65 Cf. the passages cited in Str-B 1.76-77.
66 Philo in *Mos.* 1.23 also speaks of "the Chaldean science of the
heavenly bodies." Moses acquired this from the Egyptians, "who give
special attention to astrology."
67 Jastrow 89 on אַסטגנין, אצט, אי : observer of constellations,
astrologer. The more accurate word is אַסטרולוגוס with its variants
(p. 91). Cf. also S. Krauss, *Griechische und Lateinische Lehnwörter im
Talmud, Midrasch und Targum* 2.119 and 121-122, respectively.
68 *Introduction* 96.

[i.e. punished] on account of the water of Meribah."[69]   Parallel traditions with modifications are found in *b. Soṭah* 12b[70] and *Exod. Rab.* Shemoth 1/18 on Exod 1:22.[71]

It thus seems very probable that the above Judaic comment on the astrologers' announcing to king Pharaoh that the redeemer of Israel has now been born, influenced (in an earlier form, attested in part in the variant in Josephus) Matthew's description of the magi's announcing to King Herod that the messianic king has already been born.[72]

King Herod's reaction to this announcement was to be "frightened," and all Jerusalem with him (Matt 2:3). This is based on Judaic tradition regarding king Pharaoh's reaction to being informed of the birth of Israel's liberator. Josephus for example states in *Ant.* 2.206: "Alarmed ( δείσας ) thereat,[73] the king, on this sage's advice, ordered that every male child born to the Israelites should be destroyed by being cast into the river (Exod 1:22)...." The Jewish historian adds in 215 that this child's "birth has *filled* the Egyptians *with such dread* ( δεδιότες ) that they have condemned to destruction all the offspring of the Israelites...." The sacred scribe then tells the king in 235: "this is that child whom God declared that we must kill *to allay our terrors*

---

[69] Soncino 689, which I slightly modify.

[70] Soncino 63-64, where "magicians" should be "astrologers."

[71] Mirqin 5.32, Soncino 3.25.   For the astrologers, see also *Tanḥ.* B Wayyaqhel 5 on Exod 1:15 (Buber 122, Townsend 168) and *Tanḥ.* Wayyaqhel 4 on Exod 35:30 (Eshkol 438, Berman 633), as well as *Exod. Rab.* Shemoth 1/24 on Exod 2:6 (Mirqin 5.39, Soncino 3.31), 1/21 on Exod 2:3 (Mirqin 5.35, Soncino 3.28), *b. Ber.* 4a (Soncino 10), and *Soṭah* 36b (Soncino 181). See also *Eccl. Rab.* 7:23 § 1 (Soncino 8.204) with a parallel in *Num. Rab.* Ḥukkath 19/3 on Num 19:2 (Soncino 6.749) on the astrologers of Pharaoh Neco at the time of Solomon. In Samaritan sources the chief astrologer of Pharaoh is named Palṭi. See for example the Arabic version of *Molad Mosheh* 21 and 24 (Miller 96-97, 102-103) and the Aramaic version in 11 (Miller 252-253), as well as the *Asaṭir* at 8:24 and 9:6-7 (Gaster 270 and 276, and the Aramaic in 36 and 38).

[72] Magi were also present at the miraculous birth of Cyrus, called "the Anointed One" in Isa 45:1. Cf. my study "The Magi at the Birth of Cyrus, and the Magi at Jesus' Birth in Matt 2:1-12" cited above in n. 50.

[73] Cf. LSJ 373 on δείδω, aorist.

( ἀφόβοις εἶναι )...." The king should kill him and "at one stroke
relieve the Egyptians of their *fear* ( δέος ) of him...."

In *Mos.* 1.8, Philo of Alexandria shows acquaintance with the
same motif of fear, although he lacks at this point the
announcement of the birth of the liberator of Israel. He relates
that "the king of the country, *fearing* ( δείσας ) that the settlers,
thus increasing, might show their superiority by contesting the
chief power with the original inhabitants, contrived a most
iniquitous scheme to deprive them of their strength. He gave
orders...to put the males to death...."[74]

The two first-century writers Josephus and Philo thus show
how early Judaic tradition developed king Pharaoh's reaction of
great fear or dread to both an announcement of the birth of
Israel's liberator, and to the Israelites' great increase in numbers.
This motif of fear / dread was appropriated by the Evangelist
Matthew to describe Herod's being "frightened," and all
Jerusalem with him, at the magi / astrologers' announcement to
him of the birth of the king of the Jews (2:3).

---

[74] The ultimate source of this motif may be Exod 1:12, which relates that
the Egyptians "came to *dread* the Israelites." The verb קוץ (BDB 880-881)
is employed here. For Pharaoh's arising "trembling and fearful" at
hearing the astrologer Palṭi's report of a child from Amram who will
deliver Israel from oppression, see also the Aramaic version of the
Samaritan *Molad Mosheh* 12 (Miller 254-255).

## III. Searching for the Newborn Child in Order to Destroy It, Up to the Age of Two, and Jer 31:15

When King Herod learned from the wise men / astrologers the exact time when the star of the newborn king of the Jews had appeared to them in the East, he sent them to Bethlehem, saying: "Go and 'search diligently' ( ἐξετάσατε ἀκριβῶς ) for the child." When they have "found" him, they should report this back to him (Matt 2:8). Warned in a dream not to return to Herod, the wise men / astrologers however went home by a different route. At this point an angel of the Lord appeared to Joseph, also in a dream, and instructed him to take the child Jesus and his wife Mary and to flee to Egypt, "for Herod is about to 'search for' ( ζητεῖν ) the child, 'to destroy' ( τοῦ ἀπολέσαι ) him" (v 13). When Herod then realized that he had been tricked by the wise men / astrologers, he was infuriated and "sent and 'killed' ( ἀνεῖλεν ) all the children in and around Bethlehem who were two years or under, according to the time that he had learned from the wise men / astrologers" (v 16). Jer 31:15 is then quoted.

The above three motifs of a king's "searching for," with the verbs ἐξετάζω[75] and ζητέω;[76] "destroying" ( ἀπόλλυμι )[77] and "killing" ( ἀναιρέω );[78] children up to the age of two years; as well as the quotation of Jer 31:15 in this context, all derive from Judaic comment on king Pharaoh's attempt to kill the newborn liberator of Israel, Moses.

---

[75] BAGD 275, with περί τινος : make a careful search for someone.
[76] BAGD 338-339: 1.b. look for, search someone out.  Cf. also 2:20, where an angel of the Lord informs Joseph in Egypt that "those who were 'seeking' the child's life are dead."
[77] BAGD 95: 1.a. ruin, destroy, α., esp. kill, put to death.
[78] BAGD 54: take away, do away with, destroy, α. someone, mostly of killing by violence.

## 1. Searching For

In *Mos.* 1.10, Philo notes in regard to Moses' not being able to be hidden any longer by his parents: "there were persons prying into holes and corners, ever eager to carry some new report to the king...." They were searching for newborn Hebrew males so that these could be destroyed. Josephus in *Ant.* 2.206 remarks that king Pharaoh ordered "that the labours of Hebrew women with child should be 'observed' ( παραφυλάσσω ) and 'watch kept' ( παρατηρέω ) for their delivery by the Egyptian midwives...." Moses' birth, however, had eluded the king's "vigilance" ( φυλακή - 209). God then appeared to Amram in his sleep, promising him that his child should "escape those who are 'watching' ( παραφυλάσσω ) to destroy him" (215). Finally, through the gentleness of Jochebed's delivery, she escaped "the watchers" ( τὰς φύλακας - 218).

Rabbinic sources emphasize the same motif. *Exod. Rab.* Shemoth 1/20 on Exod 2:3 for example relates that Jochebed could not hide her child Moses any longer "because the Egyptians went about from house to house, where they thought a babe had been born, taking with them a small Egyptian child and making him cry, so that the Israelite baby might hear his cry and cry with him. Thus it says: 'Take us the foxes, the little foxes, that spoil the vineyards' (Cant 2:15)."[79] Parallels are found in *b. Soṭah* 12a[80] and *Eliyyahu Rabbah* (7) 8.[81] *Cant. Rab.* 2:15 § 2 also remarks that the above verb "take" indicates that the Egyptians "watched" them for the river (Exod 1:22).[82]

The later midrash *Sefer ha-Yashar*, which incorporates numerous older traditions, also states in 67:52 that Pharaoh first decreed Exod 1:22. Then he told his servants: "Go now and

---

79 Mirqin 5.35; I modify Soncino 3.27 slightly.
80 Soncino 61.
81 Friedmann 43 on Exod 1:22; Braude and Kapstein 141.
82 Donsqi 77; Soncino 9.136-137, with n. 1. Cf. also *Exod. Rab.* Shemoth 1/21 on Exod 2:3 (Mirqin 5.35; Soncino 3.28): "Why did they cast him into the river? So that the astrologers might think that he had already been cast into the water, and would not 'search' for him." The latter is the piel of חפשׂ (Jastrow 493).

'seek' ( בְּקֵשׁוּ ) throughout the land of Goshen where the children of Israel are, and see that every son born to the Hebrews shall be cast into the river...." In 67:60-61 Pharaoh then ordered "his officers daily to go to Goshen 'to seek' ( לְבַקֵּשׁ ) for the babes of the children of Israel. And 'when they had sought' ( בְּבַקְשָׁם ) and found one, they took it from its mother's bosom by force and threw it into the river...."[83]

Both Philo and Josephus, from the first century, and the statements now found in later rabbinic sources, show that king Pharaoh's "searching for" the newborn deliverer of the Israelites in order to destroy / kill him provided the Evangelist Matthew with the material for his description of King Herod as "searching diligently" for the newborn king of the Jews in order to destroy / kill him.

## 2. Destroying / Killing the Future Deliverer

King Herod sent and "killed" all the children in and around Bethlehem who were two years or under (Matt 2:16) in order that the newborn king of the Jews might not survive. This "massacre of the innocents" is based on Judaic tradition regarding king Pharaoh's order to have all newborn Hebrew male children killed in order to rule out Moses' growing up and becoming the deliverer of Israel. Louis Ginzberg labels the latter "the slaughter of the innocents."[84]

The king of Egypt first instructed the Hebrew midwives Shiphrah and Puah (in Judaic tradition Moses' mother and sister, Jochebed and Miriam)[85] to "kill" every newborn Hebrew boy. This verb is the hiphil of מוּת in Exod 1:16.[86] When the enterprise was unsuccessful, he commanded all his people:

---

[83] Goldschmidt 241 and 242, Noach 201 and 202. Cf. Jastrow 188 on the piel of בָּקַשׁ, "to seek." For Pharaoh's guards or officers' "searching" for the newborn Moses in the Aramaic version of the Samaritan *Molad Mosheh* 22-23, see Miller 274-277.

[84] Cf. his *Legends* 2.256.

[85] Cf. the many sources cited by Ginzberg in his *Legends* 2.251, and 5.393, n. 17. The identification is Tannaitic.

[86] BDB 560: kill, put to death. The LXX has here ἀποκτείνω.

"Every [Hebrew] boy that is born you shall throw into the Nile" (Exod 1:22).[87] The latter text is the basis for almost all Judaic comment on this motif. Already in the middle of the second century BCE in Palestine, *Jub.* 47:2 mentions this motif and comments on it in v 3.[88] *Pseudo-Philo* quotes Exod 1:22 and relates the Egyptians' response to it in 9:1, his account written in Palestine about the time of Jesus.[89] In his retelling of Moses' infancy, Philo paraphrases the Exodus verse in *Mos.* 1.8, employing the verb διαφθείρω.[90] Josephus in *Ant.* 2.206 also uses the latter verb in the same context.[91] The Jewish historian employs for the same phenomenon the phrase ἐπ' ὀλέθρῳ in 2.215, and the noun ἀπώλεια in 2.225, as well as the verb ἀπόλλυμι in 2.215. The latter is the same verb used in Matt 2:13 for Herod's being about to search for and "destroy" the newborn king of the Jews in Bethlehem. Rabbinic sources also comment extensively on Exod 1:22, as shown by the examples cited in section 1. above.[92]

Today there is general consensus among commentators on Matthew that king Pharaoh's order to have all newborn Hebrew males killed lies behind the description of King Herod's "massacre of the infants" in Bethlehem.[93]

---

[87] The Samaritan Pentateuch, the LXX and the targums all add "to the Hebrews" after "is born." This is also most probably the intention of the MT.

[88] Cf. *OTP* 2.138.

[89] Cf. *OTP* 2.315.

[90] LSJ 418: destroy utterly; make away with, kill.

[91] In 2.208 he speaks of the destruction ( φθειρομένων ) of the infants.

[92] Cf. also *Sefer ha-Yashar* 68:6, "In those days the Egyptians conspired 'to destroy' ( לאבד ) all the Hebrews there," and v 11, "And Pharaoh sent his officers to take the children and 'to kill them' ( להמיתם )," in Goldschmidt 242, Noach 202. See also 67:60 cited above.

[93] This is true even if Herod is depicted as also having newborn females killed. The emphasis, however, is on destroying the newborn male deliverer of Israel / the king of the Jews. See the next section.

## 3. Children Two Years and Under in the Region of Bethlehem

Matt 2:16 states literally that Herod sent [soldiers] and "killed all the children[94] in Bethlehem and in all its boundaries from two years and below according to the time which he ascertained from the wise men / astrologers." The Greek for "boundaries" is the pl. of ὅριον, meaning region or district.[95] In translating "in and around Bethlehem," the NRSV unfortunately leaves out the twofold emphasis on "all." The author of the narrative, however, sought to accentuate the thoroughness of Herod's massacre: *all* the children, not just males like the newborn king of the Jews, in the *entire* region should be killed.

Both the motifs of "children two years and younger" and in the "region" of Bethlehem derive from Judaic comment on the infancy of Israel's deliverer, Moses.

### 3.1 Children Two Years and Younger

At the end of the Moses infancy narrative, Exod 2:10 states: "And the child grew."[96] The Hebrew וַיִּגְדַּל הַיֶּלֶד is interpreted in *Exod. Rab.* Shemoth 1/26 on this verse in light of the same phrase in Gen 21:8, which is followed by וַיִּגָּמַל : "The child (Isaac) grew, 'and was weaned.'" The midrash thus comments: "She (Jochebed) suckled him (Moses) only for twenty-four months...."[97]

The Tosefta in *Nid.* 2:1 states: "the twenty-four months in which it is normal to nurse the infant."[98] In *b. Keth.* 60a "Our Rabbis taught: A child must be breast fed for twenty-four

---

[94] The term παῖς, meaning "child," whether son or daughter, is employed in the pl. here. Cf. LSJ 1289.

[95] BAGD 581. For the region around a city, cf. Mark 7:24, "the region of Tyre," and 31a .

[96] Not as in the NRSV, "When the child grew up...."

[97] Mirqin 5.41, Soncino 3.33. This should be seen in connection with the other important links between the birth and infancy of Moses and Isaac cited below.

[98] Zuckermandel / Liebermann 642, Neusner 6.208.

months. From that age onwards he is to be regarded as one who
sucks an abominable thing; these are the words of R. Eliezer."[99]
    Early Palestinian Judaic tradition thus notes the figure of
twenty-four months or two years in regard to the end of Moses'
infancy. I propose that the author of the Matthean birth narrative
also knew of this tradition and appropriated it for the age of the
children to be killed in Bethlehem and its surroundings: two
years (Matt 2:16). By adding "and younger" the author meant to
include *all* nursing children, for they would normally only be
weaned after attaining that age. King Herod is depicted as
wanting to be absolutely sure he also kills the newborn (male)
king of the Jews.[99a] His also concomitantly killing the newborn
girls depicts him as being twice as ruthless as Pharaoh at the
time of Moses' birth, who only had the males destroyed.

*3.2 The "Region" of Bethlehem*

    King Herod's searching for the newborn king of the Jews in
the "region" of Bethlehem is based on the king of Egypt's
searching for the newborn deliverer of Israel in the "region" of
Goshen.
    An earlier Pharaoh allowed Joseph's relatives from Palestine
to settle "in the land of Goshen" (Gen 45:10), a phrase which
reoccurs frequently.[100] Goshen ( גֹּשֶׁן ) was a district or region
in Egypt in the northeast part of the Nile Delta.[101] The term
"land" ( אֶרֶץ ) of Goshen means here a district or region.[102] In
the plural it is translated in 2 Chr 11:23 ("the districts of Judah
and Benjamin") by τὰ ὅρια, the noun employed in Matt 2:16.

---

[99] Soncino 356. R. Eliezer (b. Hyrcanus) was an older second generation
Tanna (*Introduction* 77).
[99a] Sherman Johnson in "The Gospel According to St. Matthew" in *IB*
(1951) 7.261 is thus wrong in maintaining: "'From two years old and
under' indicates that the astrologers first saw the star two years before."
[100] Cf. Gen 46:28, 29, 34; 47:1, 4, 6, 27; 50:8; Exod 8:18 (Eng. 22); and
9:26. See also *Sefer ha-Yashar* 67 cited above in 1.
[101] Cf. BDB 177 and the art. "Goshen," 3., by T. Lambdin in *IDB* 2.442.
[102] BDB 76, 2.b.

Gen 47:11 speaks of Goshen as located "in the best part of the land (of Egypt), in the land of Rameses." According to Exod 1:11, part of the oppression of the Israelites in Egypt just before the birth of their deliverer Moses was their being forced to build the supply cities of Pithom and Rameses, presumably in the region of Goshen.

Bethlehem and "its entire region" in Matt 2:16 thus appears to be based on a geographical detail from the infancy narrative of Moses, born in the region of Goshen, perhaps in or near the city of Rameses. It was this region to which the king of Egypt sent his observers / guards in Judaic tradition in order to search out and kill all the newborn Hebrew male children.

### 4. *Jer 31:15*

After Herod had all the children in the region of Bethlehem killed who were two years old or younger, the author of the Matthean infancy narrative states in 2:17-18, "Then was fulfilled what had been spoken through the prophet Jeremiah: 18) 'A voice was heard in Ramah, wailing and loud lamentation, Rachel weeping for her children; she refused to be consoled, because they are no more.'"

The latter verse is Jer 31:15, generally thought to have been inserted at this point by the Evangelist Matthew.[103] Yet he cites it here because it was most probably already associated in Judaic tradition with the infancy narrative of the endangered deliverer of Israel, Moses. Matthew then only added his typical phrase of Scripture's being "fulfilled" in 2:17.[104]

The Tannaitic midrash *Mek. R. Ish.* Shirata 10 on Exod 15:20, "And Miriam the prophetess," asks on what occasion she prophesied. It was when she told her father (Amram) that he would beget a son who would arise and save Israel from the

---

[103] See the commentaries as well as the most recent study by Maarten Menken, "The Quotation from Jeremiah 31(38).15 in Matthew 2.18 : A Study of Matthew's Scriptural Text" in *The Old Testament in the New Testament. Essays in Honour of J. L. North*, ed. Steve Moyise (JSNTSup 189; Sheffield: Sheffield Academic Press, 2000) 106-125.

[104] Cf. 1:22; 2:15; 2:23; as well as 2:5 in the infancy narrative.

Egyptians. Therefore he immediately took (back)[105] his wife (Jochebed), who conceived and bore a son. When she could hide him no longer, she put him in a papyrus basket among the reeds on the bank of the River Nile (Exod 2:1-3).[106] Amram then reproached Miriam because of her prophecy. "Nevertheless she still held on to her prophecy, as it is said: 'And his sister stood afar off, to know what would happen to him (Moses)' (v 4)." Four expressions in the latter verse are then interpreted in the *Mekilta* to mean (the presence of) the Holy Spirit,[107] including "afar off" ( מֵרָחֹק ). The biblical verse cited to prove the latter is Jer 31:3, "'From afar' ( מֵרָחֹק ) the Lord appeared to me."[108] This tradition is also cited by "the Rabbis" in *Exod. Rab.* Shemoth 1/22 on Exod 2:4,[109] R. Yoḥanan in *y. Soṭah* 1:9, 17b,[110] R. Isaac in *b. Soṭah* 11a,[111] and R. Huna in *Midr. Prov.* 14:1.[112] If one had for example only the latter referent, the tradition would appear to be very late, yet it is quite old, as shown in the *Mekilta*.

The Zohar, Shemoth 12a on "And his sister stood afar off" (Exod 2:4), also quotes Jer 31:3 at this point.[113] While this writing was only completed at the end of the thirteenth century CE, its author "had expert knowledge of the early material" and sometimes "makes use of aggadot which no longer remain..., known to many medieval writers...."[114] I suggest that this is shown in the case of the following.

In 12b, R. Judah, probably III. the Patriarch, a student of R. Yoḥanan,[115] quotes regarding the daughter of Pharaoh and the papyrus basket with Moses in it: "When she opened it, she saw

---

105 On this "taking back," cf. section V. below.

106 I have paraphrased the quotation, which ends with "etc."

107 The spirit of prophecy. Cf. Jastrow 1458 on הקדש ר׳ : the holy spirit, prophetic inspiration.

108 I slightly modify Lauterbach in 2.81.

109 Mirqin 5.36, Soncino 3.28.

110 Neusner 27.47.

111 Soncino 52.

112 Buber 75, Visotzky 71.

113 Margalioth 23 or 12a, Soncino 37.

114 Cf. Gershom Scholem in the art. "Zohar" in *EJ* (1971) 16.1201.

115 Thus a third generation Palestinian Amora (*Introduction* 99).

the child" (Exod 2:6). R. Judah interprets this to mean that the Shechinah, God's indwelling Presence,[116] "hovers over Israel like a mother over her children.... 'It (the Shechinah) saw the child, and behold the babe was weeping ( בֹכֶה - v 6).'"[117] He thus renders the Hebrew of v 6a just as R. Yose b. R. Ḥanina, a second generation Palestinian Amora and older student of R. Yoḥanan,[118] does in *b. Soṭah* 12b: "She saw the Shechinah with him."[119]

R. Judah continues by stating that "The Shechinah saw the 'child,' the people of Israel, which is called 'the child of delight' (Jer 31:20), in remorseful tears, pleading with the Holy One like a child with his father...."[120]

Jer 31:20 has God ask rhetorically: "Is Ephraim My dear son? Is he the child I delight in?" It was a well-known text, read as the haftarah or reading from the prophets on New Year's in the triennial cycle.[121] The third generation Tanna R. Simeon b. Yoḥai taught ( תֿנֹי ) in regard to Isa 54:1, "Sing, O barren one," in *Pesiq. Rav. Kah.* 20/2 : "Because so many matters of moment in Israel's past go back to Rachel, therefore the children of Rachel are called by her name: 'Rachel weeping for her children' (Jer 31:15). They are called not only by her name, but also by her son's name (Amos 5:15 [with Joseph]). And even by her son's son's name: 'Ephraim is a darling son unto Me' (Jer 31:20)."[123] This is also found in *Ruth Rab.* 7/13 on Ruth 4:11 with "Rachel,"[124] and in *Gen. Rab.* Vayetze 71/2 on Gen 29:31, "And Rachel was

---

[116] Jastrow 1573 on שְׁכִינָה . The text has the Aramaic שכינתא .

[117] Margalioth 24 or 12b, Soncino 38.

[118] *Introduction* 96.

[119] Soncino 63. Notes 5-6 explain this interpretation.

[120] Cf. n. 117.

[121] Cf. *b. Meg.* 31a (Soncino 188). Often only the beginning verse of a section is cited; it was certainly more than one verse here.

[122] *Introduction* 84.

[123] Mandelbaum 312, Braude and Kapstein 332.

[124] Vilna 24, Soncino 8.90. See also R. Simeon b. Gamaliel, also a third generation Tanna (*Introduction* 85-86), with this tradition in the emended text from the current editions of *Gen. Rab.* Vayyishlach 82/10 on Gen 35:19 (Theodor and Albeck 988, with apparatus, and Soncino 2.760-761).

barren,"[125] in the name of R. Samuel b. Naḥman, a third generation Palestinian Amora in Tiberias, where R. Yoḥanan was also later active.[126]

The Tannaitic association of Jer 31:20 and v 15 noted above is reflected in R. Judah's further comment in the Zohar, *Shemoth*, which states that Miriam "went and called the child's mother (Jochebed – Exod 2:8)." The latter person "wept ( בוכה ), as it is written: 'In Rama there was a voice heard, lamentation ( בְּכִי ) and weeping, and great mourning, Rachel weeping ( מְבַכָּה ) for her children, and she would not be comforted' (Jer 31:15). It (the child) wept ( בוכה ), and the mother of the child wept ( בוכה )."[127]

Here Jochebed, the mother of the endangered future deliverer of Israel, Moses, "weeps" because of the situation of mortal danger into which she has been forced to put her infant son. R. Judah certainly draws upon an earlier tradition, as noted above, when he here associates Jer 31:20 and 15. He also continues by quoting v 9 twice.[128] Jer 31:15 is exactly the biblical verse cited in Matt 2:18 to interpret the massacre of the infants in Bethlehem,[129] itself based on the Moses infancy narrative in

---

[125] Theodor and Albeck 823, Soncino 2.653-654.

[126] *Introduction* 97 and 95, respectively.

[127] Margalioth 12b or 24, Soncino 38, which is based on a slightly different text.

[128] Margalioth 12b or 24; Soncino 38 does not have the second quotation of the verse at the very end of the unit. The catchword is again "weeping," and here Rachel is called the child's "mother" instead of Jochebed. "Ephraim is My first-born" in Jer 31:9 is interpreted of the Messiah at the time when God redeems His people in *Pesiq. R.* 34/2 on Zech 9:9 (Friedmann 159b, Braude 668). Cf. also *Midr. Pss.* 18/11 on Ps 18:7 (Buber 141, Braude 1.241). *Gen. Rab.* Vayyigash 93/12 on Gen 45:2 (Theodor and Albeck 1171, Soncino 2.868) also employs Jer 31:9 of the future redemption.

[129] While Ramah in Jer 31:15 is located north of Jerusalem, a strong alternative tradition relating it to Rachel's grave south of Jerusalem is found in Gen 35:19 ( "on the way to Ephrath, that is, Bethlehem" ) – 20 and 48:7. Zev Vilnay in his *Israel Guide* (Jerusalem: Daf-Chen Press, 1979²¹) 163 states regarding it: "Rachel's tomb, at the entrance to Bethlehem, is one of the most sacred shrines in the Holy Land."

Judaic tradition. It thus seems most probable that the Evangelist Matthew already found Jer 31:15 in the Palestinian Jewish Christian haggadic development of the Jesus birth narrative available to him. He then added his own emphasis on the Scripture's now being "fulfilled."

\*       \*       \*

The above sections I-III provide the setting in Judaic tradition for Amram's divorcing and remarrying his wife Jochebed, the mother of Israel's future redeemer. This in turn provided the background of Joseph's desire to divorce his fiancée Mary, pregnant with the future redeemer. To this I now turn.

## IV. Mary, Miriam and the Holy Spirit, and the Infants Jesus and Moses as Future Saviors

### 1. Mary and Miriam

Joseph's fiancée and later wife, Jesus' mother, is called Μαρία in Matt 1:16,18,20 and 2:11. The only other occurrence of her name in the First Gospel is in 13:55, which instead has Μαριάμ.[130] The name Μαρια (μ) in its Semitic form (see below) enabled the Palestinian Jewish Christian community which first developed a narrative of Jesus' infancy to borrow Judaic traditions on the role of Miriam in Moses' birth narrative and to apply them to Mary. This method of association is called *gezerah shawah*.[131] The Evangelist Matthew then borrowed materials from this infancy narrative for his own infancy narrative of Jesus.

Moses' older sister is always מִרְיָם in the Hebrew Bible (fourteen times).[132] The LXX consistently translates the name by Μαριάμ.[133] Josephus, a native of Jerusalem whose mother tongue was Aramaic, employs Μαριάμη twice and Μαριάμμη three times for Miriam.[134] The final η is added in Greek for the sake of declension. The targums retain the Hebrew consonants מרים, yet certainly vocalize it as in the LXX, Josephus and the Gospels:

---

130  In Luke 1:27, 30 34, 38 (twice), 46, 56; 2:5, 16, 19 and 34 (cf. also Acts 1:14) the form is always Μαριάμ. Jesus' mother Mary is thus mentioned almost exclusively in the birth narratives.

131  Cf. Stemberger, *Introduction* 21, for a description of it. It relates passages with identical expressions. One study comparing the two names is that of R. Le Déaut, "Miryam, soeur de Moïse, et Marie, mère du Messie" in *Bib* 45 (1964) 198-219. He does not relate his research to Matthew 2, however. In the Koran, Mohammed labels Jesus' mother Mary the daughter of 'Imran, the sister of Aaron, in 3:33-37; 19:27-28; and 66:12 (pp. 65, 222 and 407 in *The Meaning of the Glorious Koran*, trans. Marmaduke Pickthall). Mohammed probably took this over from tradition.

132  BDB 599, 1). See also Jastrow 843, 1).

133  It also adds it to the Hebrew in Exod 6:20.

134  Cf. Abraham Schalit, *Namenwörterbuch zu Flavius Josephus* 82 on *Ant.* 2.221 and 226, and 3.54, 105 and 4.78 respectively.

מִרְיָם. One Qumran passage reads מרים̇אם.[135] Moses' older sister
Mariam / Maryam and Jesus' mother Maria(m) thus could be
easily associated because they bore the same name.

## 2. The Holy Spirit and Mary / Miriam

Matt 1:18 states that before Joseph and Mary lived together as
a married couple, "she was found to be with child from the Holy
Spirit" ( εὑρέθη ἐν γαστρὶ ἔχουσα ἐκ πνεύματος ἁγίου ). Wishing
to divorce Mary quietly because of this seeming infidelity,
Joseph is told by an angel of the Lord in a dream: "do not be
afraid to take Mary as your wife, 'for the child conceived in her
is from the Holy Spirit' ( τὸ γὰρ ἐν αὐτῇ γεννηθὲν ἐκ πνεύματός
ἐστιν ἁγίου )" – v 20. This twofold emphasis on the Holy Spirit
in regard to Mary is due to Judaic tradition on Miriam and the
Holy Spirit. It is followed immediately by her prophecy that the
child now to be born to her parents Amram and Jochebed will
"save" Israel, the basis of Matt 1:21 (see section 3. below).

Pseudo-Philo, written in Hebrew in Palestine about the time
of Jesus, relates in 9.10 : "'And the spirit of God came upon
Miriam one night,' and she saw a dream and told it to her
parents in the morning...." The first clause is the Latin: *Et
spiritus Dei incidit in Mariam nocte.*[136] The verb *incido* means "*to
fall into* or *upon.*"[137] It is here translated via Greek from the
Hebrew original, which may have been שָׁכֵן : to rest or dwell
upon.[138] It is the same root as in the cognate noun שְׁכִינָה, the
"Shechinah, Divine Presence, holy inspiration."[139] The Hebrew
שׁכן could have been translated into Greek by ἐπισκιάζω,
"overshadow,"[140] as in LXX Exod 40:35. It should be noted that
it is the same verb employed in the Lukan infancy narrative
when the angel Gabriel tells Mary in 1:35, "The Holy Spirit will

135 Cf. "4Q 549 Work Mentioning Hur and Miriam ar" in Martínez and
Tigchelaar, *The Dead Sea Scrolls Study Edition* 1096-1097.
136 Cf. *OTP* 2.316 and SC 229.110.
137 Chambers Murray 337.
138 BDB 115, 2.c. of God; Jastrow 1575.
139 Jastrow 1573.
140 LSJ 657, BAGD 298.

come upon you, and the power of the Most High 'will overshadow' you...." The same verb may then have been translated by *incido* in Pseudo-Philo 9.10.

The late midrash *Sefer ha-Yashar*, which incorporates many earlier Judaic traditions, relates at this point (68:1) something very similar to the phrasing in Pseudo-Philo: "'It came about at this time that the spirit of God was upon Miriam' the daughter of Amram, the sister of Aaron. And she went forth and prophesied...." The Hebrew of the first phrase is ויהי בעת ההיא ותהי רוח אלהים על מרים.[141] Here the simple verb "to be" is employed of the spirit of God's "being" upon Miriam, causing her to prophesy.[142]

As pointed out above in section III. 4., the Tannaitic midrash *Mek. R. Ish.* Shirata 10 on Exod 15:20 regarding "the prophet Miriam" relates Miriam's prophecy of her father being destined to beget a son who will save Israel. This prophesying is supported by four references to the Holy Spirit in Exod 2:4, including Jer 31:3.[143] In *b. Soṭah* 11a, R. Isaac (II.), a third generation Palestinian Amora,[144] states regarding Exod 2:4, "The whole of this verse is spoken with reference to the Shechinah."[145] Here the activity of the Holy Spirit is described as the Divine Presence, His "dwelling" or "resting" upon someone. This was true both for Miriam / Maryam in the infancy narrative of Moses, and of Mary / Maria(m) in the infancy narrative of Jesus. The Holy Spirit came upon each of them.[146]

---

141 Goldschmidt 242; I modify Noach on p. 202. A parallel is found in "The Chronicles of Moses" 44:2 (Jellinek, *Bet ha-Midrasch* 2.2; Gaster, *The Chronicles of Jerahmeel* 108-109).

142 Cf. Luke 2:25 regarding Simeon: the Holy Spirit ἦν...ἐπ' αὐτόν.

143 Lauterbach 2.81-82. Cf. also *y. Soṭah* 1:9, 17b (Neusner 27.46-47) and *Midr. Prov.* 14:1 (Buber 74-75, Visotzky 71).

144 *Introduction* 98.

145 Soncino 52. A parallel is found in *Exod. Rab.* Shemoth 1/22 on Exod 2:4 (Mirqin 5.36, Soncino 3.28).

146 As Paul Billerbeck in Str-B 1.48 correctly states, however, the usage of the Holy Spirit in Matt 1:18 as "die Leben wirkende Schöpferkraft Gottes" is new; it is not found in older Judaic sources. This points to a new Christian meaning here.

In *b. Soṭah* 11b, a Tannaitic tradition relates regarding Miriam as the midwife Puah in Exod 1:15 that "she used to 'cry out' ( פּוֹעָה ) through the Holy Spirit" that her mother would bear the savior of Israel."[147] Here too Miriam is closely associated with the Holy Spirit.

## 3. *Mary and Jochebed to Bear the Savior of Israel*

After Mary "was found to be with child from the Holy Spirit" (Matt 1:18) and an angel of the Lord told Joseph not to be afraid to take her as his wife, "for the child conceived in her is from the Holy Spirit" (v 20), the angel continues in v 21 : "She will bear a son, and you are to name him 'Jesus,' for 'he will save' his people from their sins." The latter represents a wordplay in the Semitic infancy narrative source from which Matthew borrowed here. "Jesus" is יֵשׁוּעַ or יֵשׁוּ in Hebrew,[148] and the Greek "save" ( σῴζω ) is the hiphil of the same root, יָשַׁע.[149] Matthew at this point borrows heavily from the continuation of Palestinian Judaic comment on Miriam's prophesying through the Holy Spirit described in 2. above.

In the Tannaitic passage *b. Soṭah* 11b, Miriam is described as crying out through the Holy Spirit: "My mother (Jochebed) will bear a son who 'will save' Israel."[150] The Hebrew of "will save" is the hiphil participle מוֹשִׁיעַ, from the verb noted above, יָשַׁע. This form is also found in *b. Soṭah* 13b[151] and *Midr. Prov.* 31:17.[152] In *b. Meg.* 14a[153] and in *Exod. Rab.* Shemoth 1/22 on Exod 2:4,[154] Rab, a first generation Babylonian Amora who studied under

---

[147] Soncino 57. This is a wordplay between the verb פָּעָה (Jastrow 1202: to cry) and the name Puah ( פּוֹעָה ).

[148] Jastrow 599.

[149] Jastrow 601. For the wordplay, cf. the Hebrew New Testaments of Delitzsch (p. 2) and the United Bible Societies (p. 3): יֵשׁוּעַ and יוֹשִׁיעַ .

[150] Soncino 57, which I slightly modify.

[151] Soncino 65.

[152] Buber 111, Wünsche 44; it is not in Visotzky's translation, which he bases on his own version of the Hebrew text.

[153] Soncino 82.

[154] Mirqin 5.36, Soncino 3.28.

Rabbi in Palestine,[155] employs the form יוֹשִׁיעַ, even closer to "Jesus," יֵשׁוּעַ . In other similar contexts the form מוֹשִׁיעָן , "their savior," is used in the phrase "Israel's savior."[156] The basic motif is very old, as shown in Pseudo-Philo 9.10 and 16[157] and Josephus, *Ant.* 2.216.

Matt 1:21 states that Jesus "will save his people from their sins." The Evangelist formulated this on the basis of Miriam's prophecy through the Holy Spirit regarding her mother Jochebed: "My mother will bear a son 'who will save Israel,'" as in *b. Sotah* 11b above. Matthew simply substituted "his people" ( τὸν λαὸν αὐτοῦ ) for "Israel" at this point.

The Evangelist employed the same procedure for "from their sins" ( ἀπὸ τῶν ἁμαρτιῶν αὐτῶν ). In the Tannaitic *Mek. R. Ish.* Shirata 10 on Exod 15:20, for example, a variant of Miriam's prophecy as described above occurs. Here she tells her father Amram: "You are destined to beget a son who will arise and save Israel 'from the hands of the Egyptians.'" The latter phrase is the Hebrew מִיַּד מִצְרִים.[158] It is also found in the same context in the later work *Sepher ha-Yashar* 68:1[159] and in *The Chronicles of Moses* 44:2.[160] The infant Moses was later to save Israel from their bondage in Egypt.[161] Also acquainted with this

---

156 Cf. *Exod. Rab.* Shemoth 1/18 on Exod 1:22 (Mirqin 5.32; Soncino 3.25); 1/24 on Exod 2:6 (Mirqin 5.38; Soncino 3.31); *b. Sanh.* 101a (Soncino 689); *b. Sotah* 11a (Soncino 53) and 12b (Soncino 63). See also the Aramaic version of the Samaritan *Molad Mosheh* 12, where the astrologer Palti tells Pharaoh regarding Moses: "by his hand will his people be relieved ( רוח ) of all distress" (Miller 254-255), as well as Moses labeled מושיע , "deliverer / savior," in 26, 51 and 60 (Miller 282-283, 332-333 and 350-351).

157 Cf. the Latin *et salvabo populum meum*, and *liberavit per eum Deus filios Israel* in SC 229.112 and 114 (*OTP* 2.316).

158 Lauterbach 2.81.

159 Goldschmidt 242, Noach 202.

160 Jellinek, *Bet ha-Midrasch* 2.2; Gaster, *The Chronicles of Jerahmeel* 109.

161 Cf. Josephus in regard to the description of Moses' birth in *Ant.* 2.216 : "he shall deliver the Hebrew race 'from their bondage in Egypt.'" God's statement to Moses in Exod 3:10, "I will send you to Pharaoh to bring My people, the Israelites, out of Egypt," is similar and

aspect of Miriam's prophecy in the Moses infancy haggadah, Matthew simply substituted "from their sins" for the phrase "from the hands of the Egyptians."[162]

The First Evangelist in 1:18 and 20-21 thus betrays his acquaintance with, and appropriation of, motifs and phraseology from Palestinian Judaic tradition on Miriam's prophecy through the Holy Spirit regarding her mother Jochebed: she is to bear a son who will save Israel from the hands of the Egyptians. Other verses in 1:18-25 also betray Matthew's dependence on the birth narrative of Moses in Judaic tradition. To these I now turn.

---

is probably the basis of Pharaoh's assertion in *Pirq. R. El.* 48 (Eshkol 187, Friedlander 377): "In the future a child will be born, and he will take Israel out of Egypt."

[162] Here he anticipates 26:28, where he quotes Jesus as saying at the Last Supper: "This is the blood of the covenant, which is poured out for many 'for the forgiveness of sins.'" His atoning death on the Cross the next day is meant.

## V. The Marriages of Joseph and Mary, and Amram and Jochebed

Matt 1:18 states that Mary was engaged to Joseph, yet before they lived together she was found to be pregnant by the Holy Spirit. Verse 19 continues by noting that her husband Joseph, being righteous and not wanting to expose her to public disgrace, planned to divorce her quietly. Then v 20 notes that after Joseph had reflected on these matters, an angel of the Lord appeared to him in a dream and encouraged him to take Mary as his wife. When Joseph arose from his sleep, he did as the angel of the Lord had commanded him and took his wife into his home (v 24), but he did not have sexual relations with her until she had borne a son (v 25).

Almost all the marital imagery in the above verses derives from Amram and Jochebed's (re-)marriage before the birth of Israel's first redeemer, Moses, in Palestinian Judaic tradition. Before analyzing it, however, a short sketch of Palestinian marriage practices as reflected in the Matthean narrative is helpful.[1]

A girl under twelve years of age was labeled a "minor" ( קְטַנָּה ).[2]   From twelve years to twelve and a half  she was

---

[1] Cf. the sources cited in Str-B 1.45-53, 2.373-375, 393-398 and 3.376-377, as well as the articles "Marriage" in *EJ* (1971) 11.1025-1051; "Divorce" by B.-Z. Schereschewsky in 6.122-135; and "Virgin, Virginity" by Shalom Paul and Louis Rabinowitz in *EJ* (1971) 16.160-162. See also Tal Ilan, *Jewish Women in Greco-Roman Palestine. An Inquiry into Image and Status* (TSAJ 44; Tübingen: Mohr Siebeck, 1995) 65-69, 88-94, and 97-100. In a discussion of this subject with me, she asks whether Mary at her engagement and marriage could not have been older than twelve to thirteen, for example eighteen. While this cannot be completely excluded, I prefer to follow the earliest sources available to us, which I cite below. However, even if Mary was then ca. eighteen, my arguments in regard to her virginal conception remain. See also now Michael Satlow, *Jewish Marriage in Antiquity* (Princeton: Princeton University Press, 2001) 104-111.

[2] Jastrow 1350.

called a *na'arah* ( נַעֲרָה )[3] and could be betrothed / engaged
with her father's permission. As of twelve and a half years plus
one day she was considered to have come of age / be mature
and was called a *bogereth* ( בּוֹגֶרֶת ).[4] From this point on it was
thought best for her to be married as soon as possible.[5] Mary is
assumed to be a *bogereth*.

The term *'erusin* ( אֵרוּסִין )[6] signifies the first stage of
marriage: betrothal / engagement. It can also be called
*qiddushin* ( קִידּוּשִׁין ).[7] Matt 1:18 clearly states that Mary was
"engaged" ( μνηστεύω )[8] to Joseph. This engagement, however,
meant the legal relationship was already so enduring that only a
proper divorce could dissolve it.[9] No intercourse was allowed
during this period.[10] A virgin was allowed twelve months[11] to
prepare herself for the marriage ceremony proper, the *nissu'in*

---

[3] Jastrow 922. On the expression "in the house of her father...'in her
youth,'" cf. the Qumran Temple Scroll, 11Q19 53:17, based on Num 30:4
(Martínez and Tigchelaar, *The Dead Sea Scrolls Study Edition* 1272-1273).
"A young virgin who is not betrothed," based on Deut 22:28, occurs in
66:8-9 (*ibid.*, 1288-1289).

[4] Jastrow 137.

[5] Cf. *b. Pesah.* 113a (Soncino 582), where the men of Jerusalem maintain:
"if your daughter has attained puberty, free your slave and give [him]
to her." See also *b. Sanh.* 76a (Soncino 517) in regard to Lev 19:29, "Do
not profane your daughter by making her a prostitute." R. Aqiba, a
second generation Tanna (*Introduction* 79), remarks concerning this:
"This refers to the delay in marrying off a daughter who is already a
*bogereth*." Interestingly, before Pope John Paul II proclaimed the
bimillennial celebration of Jesus' birth in 2000, he proclaimed the
celebration of Mary's own birth in 1987. That is, his advisors appear to
have counseled him that Mary was thirteen when she bore Jesus.

[6] Jastrow 117.

[7] Jastrow 1355. Cf. the Mishnah tractate "Kiddushin" (Danby 321-329).

[8] BAGD 525, aor. pass. ptc. Cf. LXX Deut 22:23.

[9] Cf. the texts cited in Str-B 2.394, d.

[10] This was definitely true of Galilee. Cf. the sources cited in Str-B 1.45-
46, as well as *m. Git.* 8:9 (Albeck 3.299, Danby 319). In the latter, גוּס
does not mean to be shameless, but to be bold in the sense of being
intimate with one's fiancée (Jastrow 224).

[11] Cf. *m. Keth.* 5:2 (Albeck 3.104, Danby 251).

( נִשּׂוּאִין ),[12] when she was led to her husband's home. This is
meant by "before they lived together" in Matt 1:18, by "do not be
afraid to take Mary as your wife" in v 20, and by "he took her as
his wife" in v 24.[13] That is, Mary should most probably be
thought of as being twelve or thirteen years old at this point.
She was an 'arusah, engaged woman, and her virginity was
presupposed.

Yet Matt 1:18 and 20 state that before the second and final
stage of marriage took place, Mary was found to be pregnant.
The obligatory biblical punishment for an engaged virgin's
committing adultery was stoning (Deut 22:23-24). In the first
century CE, however, it appears that a prior warning by at least
two witnesses was required before such a drastic punishment
was enforced.[14] The woman convicted of adultery, however,
was now forbidden to her husband, being considered "unclean"
to him. The engaged man / husband was obligated to divorce
her.[15] Joseph, not willing to expose Mary to disgrace through a
public trial, with the ensuing scandal for her family, reflected on
"divorcing" her quietly (Matt 1:19).[16] The latter is the Greek
ἀπολύω.[17] It corresponds to the Hebrew גֵּרֵשׁ, the piel of גרש :
to send off, banish, especially to give a letter of divorce.[18]
Yet an angel of the Lord convinced Joseph nevertheless to take

---

12 Jastrow 909.

13 Cf. παραλαμβάνω in BAGD 619,1 : *take* one's wife *into one's home.*
See for example Josephus, *Ant.* 1.277, 302 and 17.9.

14 Cf. *Sifre* Ki Teṣa' § 242 on Deut 22 :23-24 (Finkelstein 272, Hammer
248), and *b. Sanh.* 41a (Soncino 263-265) on the latter verse. An exception
was the stoning by Zealots of someone "caught in the act" of adultery.
See my study *"Caught in the Act," Walking on the Sea, and the Release of
Barabbas Revisited* (SFSHJ 157; Atlanta: Scholars Press, 1998) 1-48.

15 Cf. *m. Soṭah* 5:1 (Albeck 3.244, Danby 298) and *b. Soṭah* 26b (Soncino
129). See also the discussion in Markus Bockmuehl, "Matthew 5.32; 19.9
in the Light of Pre-Rabbinic Halakhah" in *NTS* 35 (1989) 291-295.

16 This could be done quite simply by handing her a letter or bill of
divorce, a גֵּט (Jastrow 233). Cf. the Midrash tractate "Gittin" (Danby
307-321).

17 BAGD 96, 2.a. divorce, send away one's wife or betrothed.

18 Jastrow 273.

Mary as his wife, i.e. to take her to his home, the second and final stage of marriage (vv 20 and 24).

I shall now show how the above marriage terminology in Matt 1:18-25 is derived primarily from Palestinian Judaic tradition on the state of Amram and Jochebed's marriage at the time Miriam announces to them that her mother will bear a son who will save Israel.

### 1. *Joseph and Amram*

The Evangelist Matthew models the father of Israel's infant future savior Jesus to a great extent on Judaic tradition regarding the father of Israel's infant future savior Moses.

In *Mos.* 1.7, Philo notes regarding Moses: "He had for his father and mother the best of their contemporaries, members of the same tribe...," an allusion to Exod 2:1 with "a man from the house of Levi" and "a Levite woman."[19] Josephus in *Ant.* 2.210 speaks of "Amram, a Hebrew of noble birth...."[20] Rabbinic sources state that he was "the leading man of his generation."[21] Indeed, he was "the head of the Sanhedrin" in Egypt.[22] Other

---

[19] Philo continues by giving Moses' genealogy: "he was seventh in descent from the first settler, who became the founder of the whole Jewish nation." The reference is to Abraham. In Exod 6:14-18 Amram, Kohath, Levi and Israel / Jacob are cited, (the latter being the grandson of Abraham via Isaac). Moses as the son of Amram was thus seventh in descent from Abraham.

[20] Josephus appends Moses' genealogy in 2.229, also as the seventh from Abraham. The genealogies of the infant Moses as now found in Philo and Josephus may reflect early Judaic tradition which encouraged Matthew also to trace Jesus' descent back to Abraham in 1:1-17. Luke in contrast traces Jesus' predecessors back to Adam only after the baptism (3:23-38). For other Judaic references to Moses as seventh in line from Abraham, cf. Feldman, "Josephus' Portrait" 294.

[21] Cf. *b. Soṭah* 12a, a Tannaitic tradition (Soncino 60), and the parallel in *Exod. Rab.* Shemoth 1/19 on Exod 2:1 (Mirqin 5.32, Soncino 3.26).

[22] Cf. *Exod. Rab.* Shemoth 1/13 on Exod 1:15 (Mirqin 5.25, Soncino 3.18).

sources speak of Amram and "his court,"[23] and glorify him in other respects.[24]

Much of the Palestinian Judaic material on Amram which is relevant to Joseph is found in comment on Exod 2:1, "Now a man from the house of Levi went and married a Levite woman" (NRSV). A number of these terms and motifs are found in *b. Soṭah* 12a on Exod 2:1, which deserves to be quoted here:

> Tannaitic tradition relates: Amram was the greatest man of his generation. When he saw that the wicked Pharaoh had decreed "Every son that is born you shall cast into the river" (Exod 1:22), he said, "In vain do we labor." He arose and divorced his wife. All [the Israelites] thereupon arose and divorced their wives.
>
> His daughter [Miriam] said to him, "Father, your decree is more severe than Pharaoh's because Pharaoh decreed only against the males, whereas you have decreed concerning this world and the World to Come. In the case of the wicked Pharaoh there is a doubt whether his decree will be fulfilled or not. You are a righteous person, however, and it is certain that your decree will be fulfilled, as it is said: "You shall also decree a thing, and it shall be established for you" (Job 22:28).

---

23 Cf. *Pesiq. R.* 15/7 (Friedmann 71a, Braude 316) and 43/4 (Friedmann 180a, Braude 760), *Pesiq. Rav Kah.* 5/7 (Mandelbaum 89, Braude and Kapstein 100), and *Eccl. Rab.* 9:17 § 1 (Soncino 8.255). See also Amram's answering "the elders of the people" in regard to their decree in Pseudo-Philo 9 (*OTP* 2.315-316).

24 Cf. *b. Šabb.* 55b (Soncino 256) and *b. B. Bathra* 17a (Soncino 86-87) for Amram as one of the four who "died through the counsel of the serpent," i.e. in the Garden of Eden the serpent via Eve caused all humans to die, yet here not through their own sins. This implies Amram was sinless. See also Amram as one of the seven righteous men who caused the *Shechinah* to return to earth, in n. 32 below. In the Aramaic version of the Samaritan *Molad Mosheh* 11, Amram is described as being "one of the important men associated with Pharaoh in many undertakings. This was by reason of his great wisdom and the knowledge stored up in his heart. He was a physician in Egypt for all ailments, and God was of aid to him" (Miller 252-253). The *Asatir* in 8:38 also states that "Amram was a good physician trusted in Egypt" (Gaster 274, Aramaic 37).

He arose and took his wife back. Thereupon they all arose and took their wives back.[25]

This Tannaitic account, together with variant traditions found in the parallel passages, reflects much of the terminology and a number of the motifs incorporated in Judaic tradition on the birth of Moses which the Evangelist Matthew employed in 1:18-25. I note at this point the following seven similarities.

## 1.1 Taking a Wife

Matt 1:20 has an angel of the Lord tell Joseph in a dream not to be afraid "to take Mary as your wife." After this dream Joseph did as the angel commanded "and took her as his wife" (v 24). While this refers to the second and final stage of marriage, taking the bride to the groom's home (see above), it is based on Exod 2:1.

Exod 2:1b states that a man from the house of Levi "took" ( וַיִּקַּח ) a daughter of Levi (as his wife). That is, Amram married Jochebed. The verb לָקַח , "to take," can especially refer to taking in marriage.[26] The LXX translates it with the aorist of λαμβάνω at this point. This is the root form of παραλαμβάνω, employed in Matt 1:20 and 24.

Interestingly, MS "M" of *Targum Neofiti 1* on Exod 2:1 is thought by some to read: "(and took) for himself Jochebed his betrothed / fiancée as wife."[27] If this interpretation is correct, it reflects the two-stage marriage process described at the outset of this section. Just as Amram now took to wife his betrothed / fiancée, so Joseph took his betrothed / fiancée home as his wife in Matt 1:20 and 24.

---

[25] I slightly modify Soncino at p. 60. Cf. also the German of Lazarus Goldschmidt, 5.208.

[26] BDB 543, 4.e.

[27] Cf. A. Díez Macho, *Neophyti 1*, 2.7 with חביבתא ; the English with "his betrothed" on p. 408, n. 6; the French "sa fiancée" on p. 281, n. 2; and the Spanish "su novia" on p. 6, n. 3.

## 1.2  Divorcing one's Fiancée / Wife

After learning of his fiancée Mary's becoming pregnant, Joseph in Matt 1:19 resolved to "divorce" her. As pointed out above, the Greek verb ἀπολύω has this meaning and corresponds to the Hebrew piel גֵּרֵשׁ.

It is precisely the latter verb which describes Amram's behavior when he learns of Pharaoh's plan to cast all Hebrew male infants into the Nile. In *b. Soṭah* 12a and its numerous parallels it is related at this point that Amram concluded: "In vain do we labor (in procreation)." Then "he arose and 'divorced' ( וַיְגָרֵשׁ ) his wife," and all the other Israelites followed his example.[28]

Amram divorces his wife because of Pharaoh's intended massacre of the infants in Exod 1:22. The latter, as pointed out in section III. above, became the model for Herod's massacre of the infants in Bethlehem in Matt 2:16-18. The Evangelist Matthew creatively transferred the divorce motif from its position in Judaic tradition on Amram to Joseph. The latter desires to divorce Mary because she has become pregnant, but obviously not by him. This in turn is due to the "miraculous conception," discussed below in section 2. At this point it suffices to note that just as Amram, the father of Israel's future savior Moses, divorced his (innocent) wife Jochebed, so did Joseph, the father of Israel's future savior Jesus, want to divorce his (innocent) wife.

---

[28] Soncino 60. Cf. also *Exod. Rab.* Shemoth 1/13 on Exod 1:15 (Mirqin 5.26, Soncino 3.18); *Num. Rab.* Naso 13/20 on Num 7:43 (Mirqin 10.80, Soncino 6.550); and *Mek. R. Šim. b. Yoḥ.* Shemoth (Epstein / Melamed 6). See also *Targ. Ps.-Jon.* Exod 2:1 (Rieder 1.83, Maher 163-164). *Pesiq. R.* 43/4 employs a different verb at this point: the hiphil of יצא (Friedmann 180b, Braude 760). In the Arabic version of the Samaritan *Molad Mosheh* 22, Pharaoh orders the Israelite men, including Amram, to separate from their wives for forty days, the time within which the astrologer Palṭi predicted that Israel's savior would be conceived (Miller 98-99). The same is found in the Aramaic version, 12-13, where it is also stated that during this period Amram must remain a hostage in Pharaoh's house (Miller 254-257). The same motif of separation for forty days is found in the *Asatir* 8:30 (Gaster 272, Aramaic 37).

## 1.3  Being Righteous

Matt 1:19 states in regard to Mary: "Her husband Joseph, being 'righteous' and not wanting to expose her to public disgrace, reflected on divorcing her quietly." The term "righteous" here is the Greek δίκαιος, which in the LXX is the usual translation of the Hebrew צַדִּיק.[29] This motif of a righteous man's divorcing his own wife is based on the description of Amram in Palestinian Judaic tradition on Exod 2:1.

In the Tannaitic account in *b. Soṭah* 12a above, Amram divorces his wife Jochebed when he learns of Pharaoh's terrible decree of Exod 1:22. All the other Israelite men in Egypt follow his example. His daughter Miriam reproves him for his action, however. She states that in contrast to the doubt involved in whether Pharaoh's decree will be fulfilled, "You are 'a righteous person,' and it is certain that your decree will be fulfilled."[30]

"You are a righteous person" is the Hebrew אַתָּה צַדִּיק . It can also mean "You are righteous." This is also found in *Exod. Rab.* Shemoth 1/13 on Exod 1:15.[31]  Several other Judaic traditions also speak of Amram as being righteous.[32]

---

[29] Cf. Hatch-Redpath 330-332.
[30] Soncino 60.
[31] Mirqin 5.26, Soncino 3.18.
[32] Cf. *Mek. R. Šim. b. Yoḥ.* on Exod 2:1, "that all might know the merit of Amram the righteous" (Epstein / Melamed 6) and *Pesiq. R.* 15/7 (Friedmann 71a, Braude 316): "the righteous in your midst, such as Amram and his court." A parallel to the latter is found in *Pesiq. Rav Kah.* 5/7 on Cant 2:8 (Mandelbaum 89, Braude and Kapstein 100). See also Amram as one of the seven righteous men who brought the Shechina back down to the firmament in *Gen. Rab.* Bereshith 19/7 on Gen 3:8 (Theodor and Albeck 176-177, Soncino 1.153), and parallels in *Num. Rab.* Naso 13/2 on Num 7:12 (Soncino 6.503-504); *Cant. Rab.* 5:1 § 1 (Soncino 9.229); *Pesiq. R.* 5/7 on Num 7:1 (Braude 105-106); and *Pesiq. Rav Kah.* 1/1 on Num 7:1 (Braude and Kapstein 5-6). *Targ. Ps.-Jon.* Exod 6:20 also speaks of Amram "the pious" ( חסידא ) in Rieder 1.89, Maher 177. In light of the above texts it is difficult to understand Luz's assertion that δίκαιος in Matt 1:19 is from Matthew (*Das Evangelium nach Matthäus* 1.142, n. 9). The same applies to λάθρα in spite of 2:7 [see 1.6

It is precisely the association of being "righteous" and
divorcing one's wife in Palestinian Judaic traditions on Amram
in Exod 2:1 which provided the Evangelist Matthew the model
for his describing Joseph as "righteous" in connection with his
plan to divorce Mary. Joseph was righteous here because he felt
obligated to fulfil all the stipulations of the Torah. The latter
included the contemporary interpretation of Deut 22:23-24,
dealing with an adulterous betrothed / engaged woman.

*1.4 Divine Assurance to Joseph and Amram in a Dream*

After Joseph had considered divorcing Mary quietly because
she had become pregnant without his participation, an angel of
the Lord appeared to him "in a dream" ( κατ᾿ ὄναρ ) and
reassured him with the words: "Do not be afraid to take Mary as
your wife, for the child conceived in her is from the Holy Spirit.
She will bear a son, and you are to name him Jesus, for he will
save his people from their sins" (Matt 1:20-21). This divine
reassurance to Joseph in a dream is based on Judaic tradition
regarding divine reassurance to Amram in a dream.

In *Ant.* 2.210-216 Josephus relates that when Amram
discovered that his wife Jochebed was pregnant, he was
perplexed.[33] Therefore God appeared to him in his sleep (212),
in a vision (217), in a dream (217 - ὀνείρου ), and encouraged
him not to despair of the future (212). *"This child,* whose birth
has filled the Egyptians with such dread that they have
condemned to destruction all the offspring of the Israelites, *shall
indeed be thine* ( σὸς ἔσται ). He shall escape those who are
watching to destroy him and ... *he shall deliver*[34] the Hebrew race
from their bondage in Egypt" (215-216).

---

below] and to παραλαμβάνω [see 1. 5 below]. Hultgren in "Matthew's
Infancy Narrative" 93 incorrectly derives Joseph's being called
"righteous" from the righteousness of the patriarch Joseph, whose
influence on the Matthean narrative he also sees elsewhere.

[33] Cf. the Greek ἀμήχανος in 210: helpless, at a loss, perplexed ( LSJ
82, also on ἀμηχανάω ).

[34] Cf. LSJ 208 on ἀπολύω , 2. set free, release, relieve from, save from.
On another vision / dream that Amram has at the end of his life, see

I suggest that the Evangelist Matthew was acquainted with the same Judaic tradition reflected at this point in Josephus. He employed it, however, to describe Joseph's perplexity at Mary's pregnancy,[35] and to reassure him in a dream[36] of divine origin that he should not be afraid to take Mary as his wife, that is, also to acknowledge her child as his own. This is because the child conceived in Mary is from the Holy Spirit, i.e. a part of God's plan (1:20). She will bear a son who also will "save" or "deliver" his people (v 21).

## 1.5 Taking one's Wife Back

Because of Mary's becoming pregnant (apparently by another man), Joseph wanted to divorce her (Matt 1:19). Persuaded by an angel of the Lord in a dream not to do so, he "took her as his wife" (v 24), i.e. he performed the second and final stage of marriage by taking her to his family home. This "taking back" and performing a proper marriage act, after the stated intention of divorce, is based on Palestinian Judaic tradition regarding Amram's second marriage to Jochebed, now already pregnant with Moses.

In the Tannaitic passage *b. Soṭah* 12a quoted above, Amram first divorces his wife Jochebed because of Pharaoh's terrible decree of Exod 1:22 concerning the killing of all male children. Convinced by his daughter Miriam that, being righteous, his decree not to have children would affect both male and female

---

4Q543-547 (Martínez and Tigchelaar, *The Dead Sea Scrolls Study Edition* 1084-1093).

[35] In Judaic tradition Amram knows, of course, that he is the father of the child with which Jochebed is pregnant.

[36] The dreams of Amram (cf. Josephus, *Ant.* 2.212-217, above, and n. 34), Miriam (cf. Pseudo-Philo 9:10) and Pharaoh (cf. the sources analyzed by Renée Bloch in *Die Gestalt des Moses in der rabbinischen Literatur* 108-110) in Judaic tradition on the birth narrative of Moses certainly encouraged the Evangelist Matthew to emphasize dreams in his birth narrative of Jesus (1:20; 2:13, 19, 22). They have nothing directly to do with the dreams of Joseph's namesake in Genesis 37 and 40-41, as so often maintained, recently again by Hultgren, "Matthew's Infancy Narrative" 93.

children,[36a] Amram arose "and took his wife back." Thereupon all the Israelite men in Egypt arose and "took their wives back." The Hebrew of "and took his wife back" is וְהֶחֱזִיר אֶת אִשְׁתּוֹ. The latter verb is the hiphil of חזר.[37] The same tradition is found in *Exod. Rab.* Shemoth 1/13 on Exod 1:15.[38] Amram's taking Jochebed back, i.e. re-marrying her, is found in numerous other sources.[39] This motif is also based on Palestinian Judaic interpretation of Exod 2:1.

Exod 2:1 states: "Now a man from the house of Levi went and married a Levite woman." Since the infant Moses' "sister" (Miriam) is mentioned in vv 4 and 7, and 6:20 mentions the child Aaron before Moses, early Judaic commentators concluded that this must have been the *second* time Amram married Jochebed, Miriam and Aaron being the children from the time of their first marriage. If so, Amram must have previously divorced Jochebed. *Targ. Ps.-Jon.* Exod 2:1 expresses Amram's "taking back" or "re-marrying" Jochebed very clearly: "Amram, a man of the tribe of Levi, went and seated under the bridal canopy and (in) the wedding chamber Jochebed, his wife, whom he had divorced because of Pharaoh's decree."[40] In *b. Soṭah* 12a,

---

[36a] Miriam tells Amram, "Father, your decree is more severe than Pharaoh's. Pharaoh decreed only against the males, whereas you have decreed against both the males and females" (Soncino 60, modified). Similar imagery is found in the Passover Haggadah just before the citation of Deut 26:5. It states: "Go and learn what Laban the Syrian sought to do to our father Jacob. For Pharaoh only decreed against the male (children), but Laban sought to destroy all." See the Hebrew in *The Passover Haggadah for Jewish Personnel in the Armed Forces of the United States* (New York: National Jewish Welfare Board, 1970) 32-33.

[37] Jastrow 446: lit. to cause to return, here re-marry.

[38] Mirqin 5.26, Soncino 3.18.

[39] Cf. *Exod. Rab.* Shemoth 1/20 on Exod 2:2 (Mirqin 5.34, Soncino 3.27); *Num. Rab.* Naso 13/20 on Num 7:43 (Mirqin 10.80, Soncino 6.550); *Pesiq. R.* 43/4 (Friedmann 180b, Braude 760); *Mek. R. Šim. b. Yoḥ.* on Exod 2:1 ( Epstein / Melamed 6 ); and *Sefer ha-Yashar* 68:2-3 (Gold-schmidt 242, Noach 202). Pseudo-Philo probably means the same in 9:4-5 (SC 229.108; *OTP* 2.315).

[40] Rieder 1.83, Maher 163-164.

R. Judah b. Zebina[41] says Amram "acted towards her as though it had been the first marriage. He seated her in a palanquin, Aaron and Miriam danced before her, and the ministering angels proclaimed, 'A joyful mother of children' (Ps 113:9)."[42]

## 1.6 Quietly

Matt 1:19 states that Joseph considered divorcing Mary "quietly." The latter is the adverb λάθρᾳ, meaning "secretly," the opposite of publicly.[43] This agrees with Joseph's not wishing to expose Mary to public disgrace in the same verse.[44] The motif of "in secret," "quietly," also derives from Palestinian Judaic comment on the Moses infancy narrative, especially Exod 2:1. Three sources comment on this.

a) The first example is more general. *Eccl. Rab.* 9:17 § 1 on "The words of the wise spoken 'in quiet' are [more] acceptable" states that these words apply to "Amram and his court." A. Cohen, the translator of the Soncino edition of Ecclesiastes Rabbah, correctly remarks at this point: "On account of Egyptian oppression, they had to function in secret." Then R. Bun, a fourth generation Palestinian Amora,[45] said: "They assembled behind a stone wall or fence and argued, 'What use is there for us to marry wives and beget children whom the Egyptians cast into the river?'" Eccl 9:17b is now applied to Pharaoh, who decreed Exod 1:22. "But it was not the judgment [of God] that attention should be paid to his decree."[46]

---

[41] Str-B 5/6.179 says he was Palestinian, active ca. 300 CE.
[42] Soncino 60. A parallel is found in *Exod. Rab.* Shemoth 1/19 on Exod 2:1 (Mirqin 5.32, Soncino 3.26). In the Arabic version of the Samaritan *Molad Mosheh* 23 (Miller 100-101), Amram with the help of God impregnates Jochebed on the nineteenth day of the forty day period of separation. In the Aramaic version this is 13 (Miller 256-257), and in the *Asatir* 8:30 (Gaster 272, Aramaic 37).
[43] BAGD 462, LSJ 1023.
[44] Cf. BAGD 172 on δειγματίζω.
[45] Cf. *Introduction* 103.
[46] Vilna 50, Soncino 8.255.

The Hebrew of "in quiet" here is בְּנַחַת , "in quietness,"
"quietly."[47] Here it is Amram and his court, i.e. the Sanhedrin,
who act "quietly" or "secretly" in regard to marrying and
begetting children which could be immediately destroyed by
Pharaoh.

b) The second example applies to Amram alone, as "quietly"
applies to Joseph alone. *Pesiq. R.* 43/4 relates that Jochebed, in
spite of having already borne Miriam and Aaron, was barren for
a time when Pharaoh decreed Exod 1:22. When Amram and his
court heard of the latter decree, (as head of the Sanhedrin) he at
once ordered the Israelites not to have any more intercourse with
their wives. Thus they all divorced them, and Jochebed became
the barren woman of Ps 113:9, "rooted out of her house."

Then six-year-old Miriam reproached her father for decreeing
not only against male children, as did Pharaoh, but also against
females, and his (Amram's) decree would definitely be carried
out. Hearing this, Amram brought his daughter before the
Sanhedrin, where she repeated her argument. The members of
this body then tell him: "Amram, it was you who forbade
procreation. It is [now] up to you to declare it permitted."
Amram thereupon replies: "What do you say if I set an example
by 'secretly' bringing back [ = re-marrying ] my own wife?"
Then they ask: "But how can it be made known to all Israel?"
At this point R. Judah b. Zebida states that Amram placed
Jochebed in a bridal litter, "with Aaron on one side and Miriam
on the other carrying castanets and marching before her." This
fulfilled Ps 113:9 in regard to Jochebed. Amram did this
publicly in order that the Israelite men should know it [his
decision as head of the Sanhedrin] and thus also take back their
own wives.[48]

The Hebrew of "secretly" here is בַּחֲשַׁאי , "in secret," "in
secrecy."[49] It should be noted that Amram first wants to take
back Jochebed "in secret," but is then persuaded to re-marry her

---

[47] Cf. BDB 629 on נחת .

[48] Friedmann 180a-b; I modify Braude's translation on pp. 759-761.

[49] Jastrow 508 on חשאי .

publicly. This is Palestinian Judaic comment on Amram's "taking back" or re-marrying Jochebed in Exod 2:1.

c) Finally , the Zohar at Shemoth 19a on Exod 2:1 also relates a Tannaitic tradition ( חאנא ) that after Amram begat Miriam and Aaron, "he separated himself from his wife and then took her again."[50] In regard to the birth of Moses, Amram's name is not expressly mentioned. "Why so? Because he 'secretly' went away from [divorced] his wife and 'secretly' returned [re-married her] so that no one should notice him. Therefore it is written: 'And there went a man' (Exod 2:1); it does not say 'Amram.' It likewise says: 'And took to wife a daughter of Levi.' She also returned [re-married him] 'secretly,' therefore her name is not mentioned [in 2:1]." R. Judah (III. the Patriarch)[51] then notes that Amram himself took back Jochebed, "only his name is not mentioned because this going to rejoin his wife was not his own idea, but was inspired from above."[52]

The Hebrew of the threefold "secretly" here is בְּצִנְעָה , "in secret," "privately."[53] Here too Amram is described in regard to Exod 2:1 as re-marrying his wife Jochebed "in secret" after he had separated from her, i.e. divorced her "in secret."

---

[50] The piel of פרשׁ , to separate (Jastrow 1241-1242), is meant here as to divorce.

[51] A third generation Palestinian Amora and student of R. Yoḥanan (*Introduction* 99). Before this, R. Abbahu makes a remark. He was also a third generation Palestinian Amora and student of R. Yoḥanan (*Introduction* 98).

[52] Margalioth 19a or 36; I modify Soncino, p. 61. The Aramaic version of the Samaritan *Molad Mosheh* 13 also emphasizes divine intervention at this point. A man (an angel?) through the hand of God "the supporter" went forth and "joined Amram and Yochebed together in His glory coming down between them. And Amram knew his wife by grace. And God was the helper" (Miller 256-257). In the Arabic version (24; Miller 102-103), Palṭi the astrologer saw "that the child (Moses) had been conceived in the womb of his mother by the power of his Creator, and by the One who will make him great."

[53] Cf. Jastrow 1293 on צנעה : secrecy. With בּ , it contrasts to publicly.

The above three passages from Judaic tradition, primarily those in regard to Exod 2:1, show the background from which the Evangelist Matthew took his term "quietly," *lathra,* in 1:19. After divorcing his wife "in secret," Amram first also wanted to take her back "quietly," "in secret," but was persuaded to do so publicly. Joseph, modeled after him, also considered divorcing Mary "quietly," "in secret." The major difference is that Amram actually carried this plan of divorce out, whereas Joseph obeyed an angel of the Lord. The latter instructed him to take Mary as his wife, for the child conceived in her was from the Holy Spirit, i.e. a part of God's plan.

*1.7 Apparent Illegitimacy*

Matt 1:18 states that when Mary was engaged to Joseph, but before they lived together (stage two of the marriage process), "she was found to be with child from the Holy Spirit" and not from Joseph. That is, the child Jesus with whom Mary was pregnant at first sight appeared to be illegitimate. While I shall comment in more detail in section VII. below on later Judaic reactions to the so-called "virgin birth," at this point I shall point out that the apparent illegitimacy of the child Moses with whom Jochebed was pregnant may be a part of the broader context of Jesus' possible illegitimacy.

In *b. Soṭah* 12a on Exod 2:2, "And the woman conceived and bore a son," the comment is made: "But she had already been pregnant three months!"[54] The midrash also notes regarding "she hid him three months" *(ibid.)*: "The Egyptians counted from the time when he [Amram] took her back [through re-marriage in 2:1], while she was already pregnant with him for three months."[55] *Exod. Rab.* Shemoth 1/13 on Exod 1:15 also states concerning Amram: "he ceased to have intercourse with his wife Jochebed and even divorced his wife, though she was

---

[54] Soncino 61.
[55] Correctly translated in Goldschmidt 5.209 as "wo er sie wiedernahm." Soncino 61 falsely has "from the time that she was restored [to youth]."

already three months pregnant."[56] This accounts for Moses' apparently being born at six months[57] and for his escaping for three months the Egyptians' searching.

The above presupposes that Amram did not know that Jochebed had conceived from him just before he divorced her, and that her pregnancy was not yet visible when he re-married her three months later. In Judaic sources, pregnancy only becomes visible at three months.[58] Theoretically, Amram could have asked himself who was the father of the child with whom Jochebed was now pregnant. One late tradition even relates that after he divorced her, she married Elisaphan bar Parnak and bore him two sons, Eldad and Medad, before Amram re-married her and she bore him Moses.[59] Yet nowhere in Judaic tradition on Amram and Jochebed's marital relationship does a doubt arise on the part of Amram in regard to Jochebed's fidelity. He believes in his daughter Miriam's prophecy through the Holy Spirit that Jochebed will bear the future deliverer of Israel and he re-marries her, just as Joseph believed the message of the angel of the Lord and did not divorce Mary. For both Amram and Joseph, illegitimacy was only at first sight the case.

---

[56] Mirqin 5.26, Soncino 3.18. Cf. also the other sources cited in Ginzberg, *Legends* 5.397, n. 44. The late *Midr. Sekhel Tob* on Exod 2:2 (Buber 2.10) explicitly states that Amram did not know that Jochebed was pregnant at this point. Reference from Cohen, *The Origins* 120.

[57] On heroes being born at six (sometimes calculated as seven) months, cf. Pieter van der Horst, "Seven Months Children in Jewish and Christian Literature from Antiquity" in *ETL* 54 (1978) 346-360. In the Arabic version of the Samaritan *Molad Mosheh* 27 (Miller 108-109), Jochebed bears Moses at seven months. This is also said to be the case in the "Memar Marqah" (28; Miller 110-111), and it is repeated in the Aramaic version (15, Miller 260-261).

[58] Cf. Gen 38:24 on Tamar, referred to in Pseudo-Philo 9:5 (SC 229.108, *OTP* 2.315), and R. Meir, a third generation Tanna (*Introduction* 84), in *Gen. Rab.* Vayesheb 85/10 on Gen 38:24 (Theodor and Albeck 1043, Soncino 2.795).

[59] Cf. *Targ. Ps.-Jon.* Num 11:26 (Rieder 2.208, Clarke 220). On this Elizaphan, see Num 34:25. There is an Elzaphan son of Uzziel, Amram's brother, in Exod 6:22, which may have led to this tradition.

The above seven similarities between the description of Joseph's behavior in regard to Mary in Matt 1:18-25, and Amram's behavior in regard to Jochebed in Judaic tradition, several of them even with identical phraseology, make it very probable that the Jewish Christian Matthew employed the latter haggadic material as the background for his own portrait of Joseph and Mary's marital relationship.

### 2. Mary, Jochebed, the Daughters of Zelophehad, Sarah, Miriam and a Miraculous Conception

Before Mary lived together with her fiancé Joseph, "she was found to be with child from the Holy Spirit" (Matt 1:18).[60] That is, her conception of Jesus is described as having taken place without intercourse with her fiancé; it was miraculous. This motif of Mary's miraculous conception is influenced primarily by Judaic tradition on Jochebed, the mother of Israel's first redeemer, Moses; on Sarah and other matriarchs as conceiving without a male; and on Miriam as an ʿalmah, understood as a virgin.

#### 2.1 Jochebed and the Daughters of Zelophehad

The oldest Judaic chronology, *Seder ʿOlam*, notes in chapter 9 that Jochebed "was of those who came to Egypt, and of those who left it," after which Num 26:59 is quoted.[61] In regard to Exod 2:1, *b. Soṭah* 12a states that Jochebed was conceived on the way [to Egypt], but was born between the walls [of Egypt].[62]

---

60 Cf. also Luke 1:34-35.
61 Guggenheimer 96, with the Hebrew on p. 95; see also his note 11 on p. 98.
62 Soncino 60-61, with notes 1-3. Cf. also *b. B. Bath.* 120a (Soncino 491) and 123b (Soncino 512); *Gen. Rab.* Vayyigash 94/9 on Gen 46:26-27 (Theodor and Albeck 1180, Soncino 875); *Exod. Rab.* Shemoth 1/19 on Exod 2:1 (Mirqin 5.33, Soncino 3.26); and *Targ. Ps.-Jon.* Gen 46:27 (Rieder 1.73, Maher 151) and Num 26:59 (Rieder 2.236, Clarke 268).

*Tanḥ.* B Vaʾethanan 6 on Deut 3:23[63] and its parallel in *Tanḥ.*
Vaʾethanan 6[64] also have Moses, about to die, ask whether his
mother Jochebed should suffer sorrow also after his death. That
is, she is still alive and, in contrast to her son, now will enter the
Land (of Canaan – Israel). Judaic tradition maintains that at this
point she was 250 years old, for she was 130 when she bore
Moses (see below). He in turn was 80 when the Israelites left
Egypt (Exod 7:7), and the wandering in the wilderness lasted 40
years (Exod 16:35; Num 14:33; Deut 1:3; 2:7; 34:7) = 250.

Although she later reached the age of 250, Jochebed was
already thought to be extremely old when she conceived Moses.
Commenting on Exod 2:1, "'a daughter' of Levi," *b. Soṭah* 12a for
example asks how this is possible (for her to be called "a
daughter") : "She was one hundred and thirty years old and he
[the author] calls her 'a daughter'!"[65] Much other comment on
this verse cites the same age, as do other sources.[66] Before
Amram divorced her because of Pharaoh's decree in Exod 1:22,
she had borne him Miriam and Aaron.[67] Yet now, at 130 years of
age, Judaic tradition considered her barren, i.e. incapable of

---

[63] Buber 12, Bietenhard 2.454.

[64] Eshkol 858.

[65] Soncino 60.

[66] Cf. *Exod. Rab.* Shemoth 1/19 on Exod 2:1 (Mirqin 5.33; Soncino 3.26,
with an explanation of how her age is calculated in n. 6); *b. B. Bath.*
120a (Soncino 491); *Num. Rab.* Naso 13/20 on Num 7:43 (Mirqin 10.80;
Soncino 6.550-552, also explaining the calculation); *Targ. Ps.-Jon.* Exod
2:1 (Rieder 1:83, Maher 164); as well as *Pirq. R. El.* 48 (Eshkol 186,
Friedlander 375, with a calculation), and Pseudo-Philo 9:3 (SC 229.108;
*OTP* 2.315). The Arabic version of the Samaritan *Molad Mosheh* states
in 23: "The most amazing thing of all was that when his mother became
pregnant with him (Moses), she had reached the age of 135 years"
(Miller 100-101). Interestingly, *Test. Levi* 12:4 maintains regarding Levi:
"And in my ninety-fourth year Amram took Jochebed, my daughter, as
his wife, because he and my daughter had been born on the same day."
The Armenian MSS should be preferred to the Greek "Abraham." See
R. H. Charles, *The Greek Versions of the Testaments of the Twelve Patriarchs*
52. *OTP* 1.792 should be corrected accordingly.

[67] Miriam was thought to be six years old at Moses' birth; cf. *Pesiq. R.*
43/4 (Friedmann 180b, Braude 760). Aaron was three years older than
Moses (Exod 7:7).

conceiving a child. This was not only because her husband
had divorced her, but also because of her very advanced age.
*Pesiq. R.* 43/4, for example, has R. Samuel b. Naḥman, a third
generation Palestinian Amora,[68] maintain that Ps 113:9 applies
to Jochebed at the time Amram re-marries her in Exod 2:1 : "He
[God] gives the barren woman a home, making her the joyous
mother of children."[69] Just before this, the same text is applied to
Sarah / Sarai, who definitely was barren, for which Gen 11:30 is
quoted.[70]

At this point a "miracle" occurred to Jochebed. In *b. B. Bath.*
119b-120a, commenting on "the daughters of Zelophehad" in
*m. B. Bath.* 8:3, in turned based on Num 27:1-11, a Tannaitic
tradition states that the five daughters of this man were wise
women, exegetes and virtuous. In Num 27:1 they are
enumerated according to their wisdom, and in 36:11 differently
in regard to their later marriages.[71] In 119b, R. Eliezer b. Jacob, a
third generation Tanna,[72] states that "Even the youngest among
them was not married under forty years of age." R. Ḥisda, a
third generation Babylonian Amora,[73] then remarks that if a
woman first marries at the age of forty, she no longer can bear a

---

[68] *Introduction* 97.

[69] Friedmann 180a, Braude 759-760. Parallels are found in *b. Soṭah* 12a
(Soncino 60), *B. Bath.* 120a (Soncino 491-492), and *Exod. Rab.* Shemoth
1/19 on Exod 2:1 (Mirqin 5.33, Soncino 3.26).

[70] Friedmann 180a, Braude 758-759. For the application of Ps 113:9 to
barren Sarah, cf. also *Gen. Rab.* Vayera 53/5 on Gen 21:1, with Gen
11:30 (Theodor and Albeck 559, Soncino 1.464-465), and *Pesiq. Rav Kah.*
20/1 on Isa 54:1, "Sing, O Barren," with Gen 22:30 (Mandelbaum 310,
Braude and Kapstein 331). The Apostle Paul quotes Isa 54:1 of Sarah in
Gal 4:27. The association of the miraculous births by Jochebed (Moses)
and Sarah (Isaac) in Judaic tradition is important for the virginal
conception. See below.

[71] R. Ashi, a sixth generation Babylonian Amora (*Introduction* 107-108),
maintains in 120a that the order in Num 36:11 refers to "when one is
distinguished in old age" (Soncino 492, with notes 2-11). It should be
noted that Num 26:59, just before 27:1, names Amram, Jochebed, and
their three children.

[72] *Introduction* 85.

[73] *Ibid.* 101.

child. That is, the five women were thought to be elderly and barren.

> Since, however, they [the daughters of Zelophehad] were virtuous, a miracle happened to them as with Jochebed. As it is written, "And there went a man of the house of Levi and took to wife a daughter of Levi" (Exod 2:1). [120a] How could she be called "daughter" when she was 130 years old? ... R. Judah b. Zebida said: "This teaches that the signs of maidenhood reappeared in her: the flesh [of her body] was again smooth, the wrinkles [of old age] were straightened out, and [her] beauty returned."[74]

Here a "miracle" ( נֵס )[75] occurs to the daughters of Zelophehad, considered aged and incapable of conceiving (and thus barren), just as it does to the aged, 130 year old Jochebed. When (Amram, after divorcing her, re-marries her and) she is labeled "a daughter" of Levi in Exod 2:1, R. Judah b. Zebida, a Palestinian Amora active ca. 250 CE,[76] here notes that the "signs of maidenhood" ( סִימָנֵי נַעֲרוּת ) reappeared in her. This was the miracle: she regained the status of a *na'arah*, a girl between

---

[74] Soncino 491, which I slightly modify.
[75] Jastrow 915.
[76] Str-B 5/6.179. The name varies with Judah b. Zebina, a Palestinian Amora active ca. 300 CE (*ibid.*). Cf. the text in Goldschmidt 6.1250, with n. 87. In *b. Soṭah* 12a (Soncino 61) and *Exod. Rab.* Shemoth 1/20 on Exod 2:2 (Mirqin 5.33-34, Soncino 3.26), the latter maintains that both Jochebed's conceiving and her bearing Moses were painless. This also certainly bordered on the miraculous in light of Gen 3:16, alluded to at this point. The same assertion is made anonymously in regard to Sarah in *Tanḥ.* B Vayera 37 on Gen 22:2 (Buber 1.107; Townsend 121, with n. 134 referring to the same phenomenon in Jochebed). See also already Josephus, *Ant.* 2.218 on the gentleness of Jochebed's travail, enabling her to escape the Egyptian watchers. In *Mig.* 142, Philo describes Sarah's "bearing a son" (Isaac in Gen 21:7) as being without the aid of a midwife, an allusion to Exod 1:19, a verse also alluded to in 141. Since Exod 2:2 is alluded to in 142 (see n. "b" by Colson and Whitaker in the LCL edition), this shows that Philo also betrays a Judaic motif connection between Sarah's bearing Isaac and Jochebed's bearing Moses, important for the discussion below.

the age of twelve and twelve and a half,[77] and thus became a virgin again. Through this restoration to youth she was now capable of conceiving (with Amram's help) the deliverer of Israel.

The motif of Jochebed's miraculously now again becoming a virgin, able to conceive a child, must have been widespread, for it entered *Targ. Ps.-Jon.* Exod 2:1. This states that Amram seated Jochebed under the bridal canopy and (in) the wedding chamber after he had divorced her because of Pharaoh's decree in Exod 1:22. "Now, she was 130 years old when he took her back. But a 'miracle' ( ניסא ) was performed for her, and her 'youth' was restored just as she was when she was small (and) called 'a daughter' of Levi."[78] The Aramaic for "youth" here is עֲלֵימוּתָא ,[79] i.e. youth or her status as an 'almah, maiden, girl, entailing virginity.[80] The verb form of "was performed" is the divine passive: *God* performed the miracle of restoring Jochebed to her status as an 'almah, a girl, and a virgin.

In *b. Soṭah* 12a on Exod 2:1 it is R. Judah who remarks that Jochebed is labeled "a daughter" "because the signs of maidenhood were reborn in her."[81] He may have been a first, or

---

[77] Cf. n. 2. The Hebrew expression also denotes the signs of a girl's puberty in *b. Qidd.* 4a (Soncino 10). See also *y. Yebam.* 1:2, 3a (Neusner 21.45), with two pubic hairs. My assertion that Jochebed not only returned to her "youth," but also to actual virginity, is confirmed especially by the similar description of Sarah as a *bethulah*. See 2.2 below.

[78] Rieder 1.83; Maher 163, which I slightly modify.

[79] Cf. Jastrow 1083, who only has "strength, vigor," not meant here.

[80] Jastrow 1084. This partial explanation of the Judaic background of Mary's virginal conception (see below for the rest), excludes the suggestion made by David Daube in *The New Testament and Rabbinic Judaism* (London: Athlone, 1956) 5-9 that "God knew" (Exod 2:25 quoted in the Passover Haggadah) implies a Palestinian Judaic legend about Jochebed's conceiving Moses without the aid of Amram, i.e. he was from God Himself. Convincing reasons for rejecting this proposal are given by Hultgren in his "Matthew's Infancy Narrative" 97.

[81] Soncino 61. In the Arabic version of the Samaritan *Molad Mosheh* 24 (Miller 102-103), the restoration to "youthfulness" in Jochebed is described so: "How mistress Yochebed, when she became pregnant

possibly a fourth generation Palestinian Amora.[82] He is at any rate different from R. Judah b. Zebina, who is then quoted on Exod 2:2. The latter also cites the above tradition of Jochebed's regaining the signs of maidenhood in *Exod. Rab.* Shemoth 1/19 on Exod 2:1.[83]

God's restoring a woman to her youth, giving her again "the signs of maidenhood," including virginity, is not only found with Jochebed and the daughters of Zelophehad, as described above. It also occurred for Sarah and other matriarchs, and for Miriam. These instances most probably influenced each other in Judaic tradition.

## 2.2 Sarah

Gen 11:30 states that "Sarah was barren; she had no child." In 17:17 Abraham laughs and asks God: "Can Sarah, who is

---

with this child, grew each day in beauty, charm and stature and symmetry...." In n. 158 Miller correctly calls attention in this respect to Ginzberg, *Legends* 2.263; his n. 38 in 5.396 cites several of the relevant rabbinic sources I note above.

[82] Cf. *Introduction* 92 and 103, respectively. Since R. Hama b. Hanina, a second generation Palestinian Amora (*Introduction* 96), is cited just before this, the former is more probable.

[83] Mirqin 5.33, Soncino 3.26. Dale Allison, Jr., also notes the above texts in his *The New Moses* 147-148. Although acquainted with my study *Weihnachten...,* where I note precisely these texts in regard to the motif of "virginity" reaching Mary via Jochebed and Miriam (pp. 41-44), Allison strangely does not refer to my discussion. It is also disturbing throughout his entire study that he never cites the textual editions he employs, thus the reader not steeped in such sources cannot easily consult them. When he cites "*Tg. Exod.* 2:1," for example, he actually means *Targum Pseudo-Jonathan,* and not others; his long citation from the *Chronicle of Moses* on p. 158 is not from Gaster, *The Chronicles of Jerahmeel* 106-107, as one could assume, but is a translation of Renée Bloch's French translation in *Moïse...,* available to me as *Moses...*109, where Bloch also cites Sefer ha-Yashar, Yalquṭ Shimʿoni, and Sefer ha-Zikhronot - Allison follows her closely here; and the translation from Pseudo-Philo 9:1-2 on his p. 159 is from D. Harrington in *OTP* 2.315. Allison is also not acquainted with most of the other Judaic texts I cite in this study.

ninety years old, bear a child?" God then promises him a son,
Isaac (v 19). In 21:1-7 this birth is then described. *Pesiq. R.* 42/4
has R. Nehemiah, a third generation Tanna,[84] comment on Gen
21:1 as follows:

> "And the Lord remembered Sarah" - that is, remembered her
> with a son. As for "And the Lord did unto Sarah as He had
> spoken," Scripture means that He restored her to her youth.[85]

Her "youth" is the Hebrew נַעֲרוּת , youth or maidenhood,
the age of a *na'arah*, i.e. a girl between twelve and twelve and a
half years of age, and thus a virgin, as in the case of the
restoration of Jochebed and the daughters of Zelophehad to this
status.[86] It is to this condition that God miraculously[87] restores
Sarah so that she can conceive and bear a son. This tradition in
the name of R. Nehemiah is also found in *Gen. Rab.* Lech Lecha
47/2 on Gen 17:16[88] and in Vayera 53/5 on Gen 21:1.[89]

---

[84] *Introduction* 85. He is often in dialogue with R. Judah, as here.

[85] Friedmann 177a, Braude 744. R. Simeon b. Laqish, a second
generation Palestinian Amora (*Introduction* 94), then maintains that
since Sarah lacked a womb, God made her one. On the latter, see also
*b. Yebam.* 64b (Soncino 429, with n. 14). For the Lord's (miraculously)
"rejuvenating" ( *wa-yena'er* ) the Egyptians drowning in the Re(e)d Sea
by putting into them the strength of "youth" (*na'aruth* ) so that they
could then be deservedly punished, see the wordplay in the Tannaitic
*Mek. R. Ish.* Beshallaḥ 7 on Exod 14:27 (Lauterbach 1.246).

[86] Cf. n. 2.

[87] This is expressly labelled a "miracle" ( נִיסָא ) in *Targ. Ps-.Jon.* Gen
21:1 (Rieder 1.28, Maher 74). *Neophyti 1* even increases this to the plural,
"miracles" (Díez Macho 1.117 and 547 , McNamara 112). Cohen in *The
Origins* 144 points out how Rashi in his commentary on *b. Soṭah* 12a
closely connects the miraculous restoration of Jochebed to her condition
as a *na'arah* with a menstrual cycle, and "the miracle of Sarah
conceiving Isaac (Gen. 18.11)."

[88] Theodor and Albeck 472, Soncino 1.400.

[89] Theodor and Albeck 559, Soncino 1.465. Martin Dibelius in
*Jungfrauensohn und Krippenkind. Untersuchungen zur Geburtsgeschichte
Jesu im Lukas-Evangelium* (Heidelberg: Carl Winter, 1932) 28 had
called attention to the latter two passages in another respect.

The *Fragment Targum*, MS "V," on Gen 18:11 also has Sarah ask: "After I have grown old, is it possible to return to the days of 'my youth' ( טל יותי ) and become pregnant – and Abraham is old?"[90] The answer is of course yes, with God's aid. In *Gen. Rab.* Vayera 48/19 on Gen 18:14, "Is anything too hard for the Lord?" R. Yudan (Judah) b. R. Simon, a fourth generation Palestinian Amora,[91] has God remark on this verse in regard to Abraham and Sarah: "I can create man from the beginning [*de novo*], yet [you would say that] I cannot restore them to their youth?"[92] The same rabbi comments in 48/17 on Gen 18:12 by having God ask in regard to Abraham and Sarah in v 13: "'I am too old' to perform miracles ( ניסים )?"[93] Here God's restoration of Sarah from old age to her youth, including virginity, is considered a "miracle."[94]

In *b. B. Meṣiʿa* 87a R. Meir, a third generation Tanna,[95] comments on Abraham's taking butter, milk and a calf, but no bread to offer in hospitality to the three men who visit him in Gen 18:1-5 : "that day our mother Sarah had her menstrual period."[96] H. Freedman notes on this: "And so defiled the bread she had baked. As she was already old, the phenomenon was an earnest of the rejuvenation which was to make the birth of Isaac

---

[90] Klein 1.137 and 2.100. Cf. Jastrow 537 on טל יות : childhood, youth.

[91] *Introduction* 103, and Str-B 5/6.200.

[92] Theodor and Albeck 495 with "to the days of their youth," and Soncino 1.418.

[93] Theodor and Albeck 494, Soncino 1.417. The same rabbi in 53/6 on Gen 21:1 (Theodor and Albeck 560, Soncino 1.466) states that Sarah had no need for sexual desire, for God "in His glory" [made her conceive].

[94] Cf. also the targumic texts on Gen 21:1 cited in n. 87. The situation of Zechariah and Elizabeth, both old and she also barren (Luke 1:7, 18, 38), yet who conceived a son, John, "for nothing will be impossible with God" (v 37), appears to be modelled on Abraham and Sarah in Judaic tradition. It cannot be emphasized enough that the narrative is interwoven with Mary's virginal conception (vv 34-35).

[95] *Introduction* 84.

[96] Soncino 501. Cf. the parallel in *Gen. Rab.* Vayera 48/14 on Gen 18:8 (Theodor and Albeck 490-491, Soncino 1.414), as well as *Pirq. R. El.* 36 (Friedlander 275).

possible."[97] Finally, in the same section R. Ḥisda, a third generation Babylonian Amora,[98] comments on Sarah's stating in Gen 18:12, "After I have waxed old, I have had youth," in the following way: "After the flesh is worn and the wrinkles have multiplied, the flesh [of Sarah] was rejuvenated, the wrinkles were smoothed out, and beauty returned to its place."[99] This is almost the same description as is made of Jochebed in *b. B. Meṣ.* 120a (see above) when God restores her to her youth, including virginity, so that she can bear Moses, the future redeemer of Israel. It appears to have been a floating tradition in regard to precisely such women, similar to both Jochebed's and Sarah's conceiving and giving birth painlessly, as noted above.

*Eliyyahu Rabbah* (5) 6 also maintains that Abraham and Sarah, though now old and white-haired, became young again. They both returned to their "youth" ( יַלְדוּת ).[100] On Abraham's coins the one side showed them as an old man and an old woman. The other side had their images as a "young man" or "youth" ( בָּחוּר )[101] and a "virgin" ( בְּתוּלָה ). The latter term definitely means a return to Sarah's physical virginity.[102] This tradition[103]

---

[97]  Soncino 501, n. 8.

[98]  *Introduction* 101.

[99]  Soncino 502. Cf. the Hebrew text in Goldschmidt 6.787.

[100] Jastrow 578: childhood, youth.

[101] Jastrow 154-155, 2).

[102] Jastrow 200: "untouched." He cites *b. Yebam.* 61b (Soncino 410), where a Tannaitic tradition explains a *bethulah* in the legal sense as a *na'arah*, that is, between twelve and twelve and a half years old (see n. 3) – and by definition a virgin. The Tosefta at *Šebi'it* 3:15 (Zuckermandel and Liebermann 65, Neusner 1.217) states that "A virgin woman is any [woman] who has never before had intercourse."

[103] Cf. Friedmann 28-29, and Braude and Kapstein 104-105. Before this, after a quotation of Gen 18:11, "Now Abraham and Sarah were old," the text explicitly states: "Sarah became [again] like a virgin (*bethulah*)" (Friedmann 28).

is also found in *Gen. Rab.* Lech Lecha 39/11 on Gen 12:2,[104] and in *b. B. Qam.* 97b.[105]

Sarah's divine restoration from an old woman to a "virgin" in Palestinian haggadic tradition (in an earlier stage) may have influenced Philo's depiction of Sarah's giving birth to Isaac, often held to be of relevance to the "virgin birth" of Jesus.

In *Cher.* 40-52 (XII-XV) the Alexandrian contemporary of Jesus maintains that Abraham, Isaac, Jacob and Moses did not know women, i.e. have sexual relations with them (40). Their wives Sarah, Rebecca, Leah and Zipporah were rather "virtues" (ἀρεταί - 41). The mode of their conceiving and having birth pangs, Philo maintains, belongs to the realm of a "divine mystery" ( θείας...μύστας), only available to "the initiated who are worthy to receive 'the holiest secret' ( τῶν ἱερωτάτων - 42)." It is God Himself who sows in the virtues the good seed (44). Since Abraham is not mentioned in Gen 21:1, the Alexandrian philosopher can assert that Moses "shows us Sarah conceiving at the time when God visited her in her solitude," yet she brought forth to Abraham (45).[106]

Only the purified ears of the initiated can receive such "holy mysteries" ( ἱερὰ...μυστήρια - 48).[107] Philo connects God

---

[104] Theodor and Albeck 374, Soncino 1.320. H. Freedman translates here as "a girl," but Jastrow (155 on *baḥur* ) more precisely as "a virgin."
[105] Soncino 567-568. Isaac and Rebecca are not meant by the second side of the coins, as maintained in n. 2, but Abraham and Sarah restored to their youth.
[106] Cf. F. H. Colson's note in the LCL edition, II. 483: "'In her solitude.' Apparently a fanciful deduction from the fact that Abraham's presence is not mentioned in Gen. xxi.1. In the cases that follow there is the same deduction from the absence of any mention of the husband." See also *All. Leg.* 3.218-219 for the Lord's "begetting" Isaac, and *Mut.* 131 for Isaac as "a son of God." Erwin Goodenough in *By Light, Light: The Mystic Gospel of Hellenistic Judaism* (New Haven: Yale University Press, 1935) 155 cites the latter passages and speculates that Christian copiests may have suppressed a treatise *De Isaaco* because Isaac was presented there "as the son of God by a virgin." Goodenough is followed here by Kensky, "Moses and Jesus" 46-47, and 49. Unfortunately, this must remain speculative.
[107] In 49 they are called Moses' "great mysteries."

as described in his Greek version of Jer 3:4 to these: "Did you
not call upon Me as your house, father and 'the husband of your
virginity' ( ἄνδρα τῆς παρθενίας σου )?" (49). When "God
begins to consort with the soul, He makes what  before was a
woman 'into a virgin again'...." He only speaks with Sarah
when she "is ranked once  more as a pure virgin" (50). The
Greek of "into a virgin again" here is παρθένον αὖθις.[108] It is
exactly the same motif of God's "restoring" Sarah to her physical
"virginity" as noted in the Palestinian haggadic sources cited
above. Philo continues by emphasizing that God is the husband
of "virginity," as in Jer 3:4 (51),[109] and he stresses the virgin
virtues (52).

In this section of *Cherubim* Philo shows that he is dependent
on earlier tradition.[110] Only those properly initiated (into the

---

[108] Cf. LSJ 276 on the latter word:  again, anew. See also *Cong.* 7
regarding Sarah, for whom God opens the womb "which yet loses not
its virginity." On God's changing "old age into youth" in regard to
Abraham and Sarah, which is miraculous, see *Questions and Answers on
Genesis* 3.56 on Gen 17:17 (LCL Supplement I. 257), as well as Philo's
comment in 3.18 on Gen 15:1 (*ibid.*, I. 202-203).

[109] Cf. F. H. Colson's note in the LCL edition, II. 483, on the "husband"
as lacking in the LXX, thus Philo "may be quoting some earlier
rendering." For an unclear passage regarding (God's) "begetting" the
Messiah at a gathering of the community council in Qumran, see 1Q28a
(1Qsa) 2:11-12 (Martínez and Tigchelaar, *The Dead Sea Scrolls Study
Edition* 102-103).

[110] Correctly seen by Eduard Norden in *Die Geburt des Kindes.*
*Geschichte einer religiösen Idee* (Darmstadt: Wissenschaftliche
Buchgesellschaft, 1969; original in Studien der Bibliothek Warburg III,
1924) 78, n. 3. Yet Norden himself says Philo derives it from "Greek-
Egyptian theosophy" (p. 79). He also falsely maintains that virginity in
a religious sense was unknown to Judaism (p. 80). Norden notes on
p. 78 that H. Leisegang had already called attention to the *Cherubim*
passages in his *Pneuma Hagion* (Leipzig, 1922) 43ff. In his *Jungfrauensohn
und Krippenkind* 34, Martin Dibelius also analyzes the *Cherubim*
passages and more correctly concludes that Hellenistic Judaism derived
the miraculous birth of famous people, without a human father, from
God. Dibelius believes that the phrase "born according to the Spirit" in
Gal 4:29 points to the same phenomenon in Hellenistic Judaism (30),
which is doubtful. On this, see the commentaries. See also Walter Radl,

teachings of the Alexandrian Jewish community) can receive such "holy mysteries." The latter include the non-LXX rendering of Jer 3:4 with God as "the husband of your virginity," i.e. Sarah's conception of Isaac takes place without Abraham after God has made her into a virgin (*parthenos*) again. One can thus rightly speak of this as a miraculous, virginal conception, even if Philo clothes the entire passage in flowery, allegorical language.[111]

It is known that there was a pre-Christian synagogue of the Alexandrians in Jerusalem.[112] As pointed out by Martin Hengel and others in recent decades, much more contact between Hellenistic, primarily Alexandrian, and Palestinian Judaism took place than was earlier presupposed. One cannot thus maintain that Sarah's virginal conception of Isaac as now found in Philo, our earliest extant source for this motif, caused Palestinian Judaism to adopt a very similar motif, as shown in Sarah's coinage depicting God's restoring her to the state of a "virgin," and in the third generation Tanna R. Nehemiah's remarks on this subject. The development of this motif may – and I think more probably – have developed in the motherland and only then have spread to the diaspora, where it was further developed: after the woman's restoration to virginity, she was described as conceiving not from her husband by marriage, but from God as her husband. Regardless of whether this motif was basically originally Palestinian or Alexandrian-Hellenistic Jewish, its early date in both sections of Judaism is attested by a contemporary of Jesus, Philo, and by one of the earliest Tannaim of whom we have record, R. Nehemiah.

---

*Der Ursprung Jesu*. Traditionsgeschichtliche Untersuchungen zu Lukas 1-2 (Herders Biblische Studien 7; Freiburg: Herder, 1996) 356-357, on the Philonic passages. Radl favors here the influence of ancient Egyptian mythology in regard to the birth of Pharaoh as a divine king (357-360).

[111] Although he reaches a different conclusion, cf. also the careful study of the Philonic passage by Pierre Grélot, "La naissance d'Isaac et celle de Jésus: Sur une interprétation 'mythologique' de la conception virginale" in *NRT* 94 (1972) 462-487 and 561-585.

[112] Cf. Acts 6:9 and the passages cited in Str-B 2.663-664.

For the above reasons I suggest that the probably much better known idea of God's restoration of the elderly Sarah to a state of youth, including virginity, influenced in Palestinian Judaic sources the description of God's restoring the elderly Jochebed to a state of youth, including virginity. Only in this restored state could Sarah conceive Isaac through intercourse with Abraham; only in this restored state could Jochebed conceive the future redeemer of Israel, Moses, through intercourse with Amram. Writing in Greek also to Hellenistic Jewish Christians and to Gentiles, the Evangelist Matthew borrowed the more elaborate form of this motif from Hellenistic Judaism as already found in his own (in part Hellenistic) Jewish Christian community in order to describe the virgin Mary's conceiving Jesus without first having intercourse with her fiancé / husband Joseph. In Alexandrian Judaism it was not Abraham who was depicted as the father of Isaac, but God Himself. Matthew employs this same phenomenon by stating that Mary was found to be with child from the Holy Spirit, i.e. the Spirit of God (1:18, 20). Jesus is thus of divine origin (1:23, "God with us"; 2:15, "My Son"). The fact that the Evangelist Luke employs the same motif in 1:34-35, including Jesus as "Son of God," shows that he too lived in, or derived it from, a Christian community which was influenced by Hellenistic Jewish Christians acquainted with the phenomenon of a "virginal conception." Both evangelists drew upon a tradition which had already been formulated in their respective communities.

*2.3 Miriam*

Palestinian Judaic tradition also maintained that God later restored Miriam to the status of youthfulness, including virginity, allowing her to conceive and bear a child. To understand this properly, several remarks on the Judaic understanding of Chronicles are helpful.

In *Ruth Rab.* 2/1 Rabbi or Judah the Prince, a fourth generation Tanna,[113] states: "The book of Chronicles was given

---

[113] *Introduction* 89.

only for purposes of [midrashic] interpretation."[114] The Soncino English translator L. Rabinowitz explains this as follows: "Chronicles, especially the genealogical lists at the beginning, are not to be understood literally, but allegorically."[115] The same statement made by Rabbi is given in the name of Rab, a first generation Babylonian Amora,[116] in *Lev. Rab.* Vayyikra 1/3, where the name "Hajehudijah" in 1 Chr 4:18 is interpreted of Jochebed.[117] Finally, in *b. Meg.* 13a, R. Simon b. Pazzi, a third generation Palestinian Amora,[118] "once introduced an exposition of the Book of Chronicles as follows: 'All thy words are one, and we know how to find their meaning.'" The Soncino English translator M. Simon explains this by stating that "numerous names in the Book of Chronicles refer to the same person."[119] The names of 1 Chr 4:18 are then interpreted in light of Exod 2:5 as names of Moses. This Palestinian Judaic view of Chronicles aids in understanding the following passage concerning Miriam.[120]

*Exod. Rab.* Shemoth 1/17 deals with Exod 1:21, which states that "because the midwives feared God, He built them houses." The midwife Puah was interpreted as Miriam,[121] and here the opinion is given that "a royal family [thus 'house,' came] from

---

[114] Vilna 6, Soncino 8.23.

[115] Soncino 8.23, n. 1.

[116] *Introduction* 93.

[117] Mirqin 7.11, Soncino 4.4.

[118] *Introduction* 99.

[119] Soncino 74, with n. 3.

[120] The Tannaitic midrash *Sifre* Beha'alothecha § 78 on Num 10:29-36 (Horovitz 74-75, Neusner 2.58-59) also deals with the "houses" of Exod 1:21 and attributes the royal house to Miriam. She is the Aharhel of 1 Chr 4:8 and the Ephrath of 2:19, from whom David descended. The figurative interpretation of the names in Chronicles was thus definitely already Tannaitic. For Mary's also being of Davidic descent, cf. the variant MS traditions on Luke 2:4; Ignatius, *Eph.* 18:2 (LCL 1.190-193); Justin's "Dialogue with Trypho" 43:1, 45:4, 100:3 (Marcovich 140, 144 and 241-243; *The Ante-Nicene Fathers* 1.216, 217, 249); the Protevangelium of James 10:1 (Schneemelcher, *New Testament Apocrypha* 1.430); *Mart. Isa.* 11:2 (*OTP* 2.174); and perhaps *b. Sanh.* 106a in section VII. b) below.

[121] Cf. for example 1/13 on Exod 1:15 (Mirqin 5.25, Soncino 3.17).

Miriam because David descended from Miriam." She is the
"Azubah" of 1 Chr 2:18, called so because "all had forsaken
her."[122] The phrase "And Azubah died" in v 19 is taken to mean
that "she was ill and was treated as if already dead, [her
husband] Caleb too forsaking her." "Caleb married 'Ephrath'"
in the same verse is also explained to mean he married Miriam.
"And he took unto him" [ = he married ] means that "when she
was healed, he treated her as though he were now marrying her,
placing her in the [marriage] litter, on account of his great joy in
her." This recalls Amram's treatment of Jochebed when he re-
married her in Palestinian Judaic interpretation of Exod 2:1.

   The midrash continues by quoting 1 Chr 4:5, "Ashhur father
of Tekoa had two wives, Helah and Naarah." "Ashhur" is Caleb,
and the latter two names both mean Miriam. This is because
Miriam "was ill and she bestirred herself in spite of her illness,
and the Holy One, blessed be He, 'restored her to her youth,
[including virginity].'" Then she recovered from her sickness
(which had made her barren), and bore her husband children.[123]
The last phrase quoted is the same as that employed of Jochebed,
the daughters of Zelophehad, and Sarah above.

   It is thus not only the "miracle" which occurred to aged
Jochebed, enabling her to regain the status of a *na'arah*, including
virginity, and to conceive from Amram a son, Moses, who
would become the future deliverer of Israel, which influenced
the Palestinian Jewish Christian account of Jesus' "miraculous
conception" through the Holy Spirit. It was also Palestinian
Judaic tradition on Miriam, upon whom the Holy Spirit rested
and made her prophesy that her mother would bear the future
deliverer of Israel. She was restored to the status of a *na'arah*

---

122 A wordplay on עֲזוּבָה and the verb עָזַב , meaning to leave,
abandon (Jastrow 1060, 2).

123 Mirqin 5.30-31, Soncino 3.22-24. There is a wordplay between the
name חֶלְאָה and "being ill," חלה (Jastrow 467), and another between
the name נַעֲרָה , "bestirring oneself," the niphal of נער (Jastrow 921),
and "youth," נַעֲרוּת . Much of the material in *Exod. Rab.* Shemoth 1/17
is also found in *b. Soṭah* 11b-12a (Soncino 58-59). See also *Tanḥ.* B
Vayyeṣa 10 on Gen 29:31 (Buber 1.152; Townsend, Genesis 185;
Bietenhard 1.165).

(cf. her name Naarah in 1 Chr 4:5 above), including virginity, enabling her to conceive from her husband and bear a child. The emphasis on Miriam / Maryam's restored virginity thus may also have aided Matthew (or the Jewish Christian community behind him) in emphasizing Mary / Miriam / Maryam's virginity.

Further Judaic comment on Miriam as an ʿ*almah* ( עַלְמָה ) should also be analyzed, for it most probably encouraged the Evangelist to quote Isa 7:14 in Matt 1:23 and to describe Mary as a "virgin" even after she conceived Jesus.

In Exod 2:3-4 Jochebed placed Moses in a papyrus basket among the reeds of the Nile, with Miriam looking on from a distance to see what would happen to the baby. Judaic comment on this incident is very old, as shown in the Palestinian writing *Jubilees*, originally in Hebrew from ca. 150 BCE. In 47:4 it comments on Exod 2:4 in an haggadic manner by stating regarding Moses: "your mother came in the night and suckled you, and (in) the day Miriam, your sister, guarded you from the birds."[124]

At this point Pharaoh's daughter discovered the baby Moses. Miriam then asked her whether she should go and get a Hebrew woman to nurse it. When the reply was positive, "the 'girl' went and called the child's mother" (Exod 2:8), who then nursed it. The Hebrew for "girl" here is עַלְמָה , meaning "lass," "maiden," or "young woman."[125] The LXX translates it by νεᾶνις , "girl, maiden."[126] The unusual Hebrew called forth much Judaic comment.

Already in the second century BCE, in his Greek drama "The Exodus" Ezekiel the Tragedian, perhaps writing in Alexandria, described the above scene at the end of what is now fragment one. Moses there relates:

> And then said my sister Miriam as she *ran* to the princess,
> "Do you want me *quickly* to find you a nurse for this child from
> the Hebrews?" And she *hastened* the girl on her way. She went

---

124 *OTP* 2.138.
125 Jastrow 1084, BDB 761.
126 LSJ 1164.

and told her mother, and *right away* came my mother and took me in her arms.[127]

The above italicized words all interpret the ʿalmah of Exod 2:8. She "ran" is from προστρέχω,[128] "quickly" and "right away" are ταχύ,[129] and "hastened" is the Greek ἐπισπεύδω.[130] They are all based on the underlying cognate verb of ʿalmah: עָלַם , Aramaic עֲלַם , עָלְ ים , to be strong.[131] This becomes clear from the rabbinic sources I cite below.

In *Mos.* 1.12 Philo deviates from the LXX, which he usually follows, and states that Miriam at this point is ἔτι παρθένος , "still a maiden / girl."[132] In 1.16 he employs the same verb as in Ezekiel the Tragedian, προστρέχω : "The child's sister...*ran up* from where she stood like a scout...." In *Ant.* 2.227 Josephus relates that "the princess bade her [Miriam] do this service herself and *run for* a foster-mother." The Jewish historian from Jerusalem employs the verb μεταθέω here.[133]

In *b. Soṭah* 12b on Exod 2:8, R. Eleazar (b. Pedat, a third generation Palestinian Amora)[134] says: "It ( ha- ʿalmah ) teaches that she went quickly like a young woman."[135] "Quickly" is the

---

[127] This English translation with the original Greek is from Carl Holladay, *Fragments from Hellenistic Jewish Authors*, Vol. II, Poets, 350-351, with information on the writing on pp. 302 and 312. Cf. also *OTP* 2.803-804, with the text on p. 809.

[128] LSJ 1528: *run to* or *towards*.

[129] LSJ 1762: swiftly, quickly.

[130] LSJ 658: urge on, hasten.

[131] Jastrow 1084.

[132] LSJ 1339. F. H. Colson in the LCL translation has "a girl still unmarried," which to the modern reader is misleading in the context.

[133] LSJ 1112. In 221 he passes on the haggadic tradition that at her mother's bidding, Miriam "kept pace" with the basket of papyrus reeds to see where it would go. That is, it is not thought of as remaining in one place in the reeds along the shore, but as being carried along by the water. See ἀντιπαρέξειμι (LSJ 160) as to proceed in a parallel direction, similar to ἀντιπάρειμι : to march on opposite sides of a river (*ibid.*).

[134] *Introduction* 98, which says he died in 279 CE.

[135] Soncino 65, with n. 4. The Aramaic version of the Samaritan *Molad Mosheh* 24 (Miller 278-279) states that Pharaoh's daughter, whose

Hebrew בְּזְרִיזוּת , with "strength," "quickness."[136] "Like a young woman" is "like an *'almah*." Since Judaic tradition thought of Miriam as only six years old here,[137] it emphasizes the child's quickness, as if she were at least double her age and much stronger. This is the explanation for Miriam's "running" "quickly" in Ezekiel the Tragedian, Philo and Josephus above.

Another wordplay with *'almah* in Exod 2:8 is made by R. Samuel b. Naḥman, also a third generation Palestinian Amora,[138] in *b. Soṭah* 12b. He maintains Miriam is labeled so "because she made the words secret." The Soncino translator A. Cohen notes here: " *'Almah* means 'to hide'; she did not disclose her relationship to the child."[139]

The above Judaic comment on Miriam as an *'almah* in Exod 2:8, attested already in Ezekiel the Tragedian, and then in Philo and Josephus, as well as in later rabbinic sources, shows how easily the mother of Israel's final redeemer, the Messiah Jesus, could also be described as an *'almah*. Such comment could have reinforced the transfer of the motif of virginity ( *'almuth*, youth, including virginity) by the bilingual Jewish Christian community from which Matthew came (Antioch, or perhaps Damascus in

---

sickness was "quickly" healed when she touched the baby Moses, "sent and called 'in a hurry' for a nurse to give suck to the child." When Moses refused an Egyptian wet nurse, Miriam "went 'quickly' to Pharaoh's daughter and said to her, 'Shall I go and call a nurse from the Hebrew women?' And Pharaoh's daughter said to her, 'Go quickly.'" Here the motif of "quickly" is emphasized four times. In regard to Exod 2:7, the *Asatir* at 9:11 says Miriam "ran" to Pharaoh's daughter and asked her, "Shall I go..." (Gaster 276; his note *ad loc.* should be corrected to "II, 7").

[136] Jastrow 413 on זְרִיזוּת .

[137] Cf. *Pesiq. R.* 43/4 (Friedmann 180b, Braude 760), as well as *Exod. Rab.* Shemoth 1/13 on Exod 1:15 for Miriam as five years old a year before (Mirqin 5.25, Soncino 3.16, with n. 1 on p. 17). See also Jochebed's statement about Miriam in the latter passage: "She is only a child and knows nothing" (Soncino 3.17).

[138] *Introduction* 97.

[139] Soncino 65, with n. 5. See Jastrow 1084 on the hiphil of עָלַם II. A parallel to both statements is found in *Exod. Rab.* Shemoth 1/25 on Exod 2:8 (Soncino 3.32, with notes 5-6).

Syria?) from Miriam / Maryam in the Moses birth story in Judaic tradition, to Mary / Miriam / Maryam in the Gospel birth story. The Hebrew catchword ʿ*almah* also inspired the Evangelist to quote Isa 7:14 in Matt 1:23. The Hebrew text of Isaiah also has ʿ*almah* here, and it is one of only four occurrences in the MT of the noun in the singular.[140] Except for changing καλέσεις into καλέσουσιν, Matthew here closely follows the LXX, including ἡ παρθένος for ʿ*almah*. In light of Mary's conceiving not by Joseph but by the Holy Spirit (1:18 and 20), Matthew definitely intended the term ἡ παρθένος in LXX Isa 7:14 to be understood as the "virgin," and not in its original meaning as "young woman," or (marriageable) "maiden."[141] He himself interpreted the Isaian passage to be a prediction of Jesus' birth by the "virgin" Mary.[142]

---

140 Cf. Gen 24:43, Exod 2:8, and Prov 30:19. The plural is found in Ps 68:26 (Eng. 25), Cant 1:3 and 6:8. Playing "according to Alamoth" is found in 1 Chr 15:20, Ps 9:1 (corrected), and 46:1. The plural in Ps 48:15 means "forever." Maarten Menken in "The Textual Form of the Quotation from Isaiah 7:14 in Matthew 1:23" in *NovT* 43 (2001) 144-160 maintains instead that Matthew quotes Isa 7:14 from a revised form of the LXX which betrays an attempt to better render the Hebrew.

141 Cf. the Isaiah commentaries such as Georg Fohrer, *Das Buch Jesaja* (Zürcher Bibelkommentare; Zurich / Stuttgart: Zwingli Verlag, 1966²) 1.111, n. 53, and Hans Wildberger, *Jesaja* (BKAT 10; Neukirchen: Neukirchener Verlag, 1980²) 1.290. In his commentary *Matthew. A Commentary on His Handbook for a Mixed Church under Persecution* (Grand Rapids, MI: Eerdmans, 1994²) 25, Robert Gundry maintains in contrast that Isaiah prophesied here regarding the virginal conception and birth of the "divine child Jesus." In his *The Use of the Old Testament in St. Matthew's Gospel* (Supp. NovT 18; Leiden: Brill, 1967) 195, Gundry states that Isa 7:14 is "introduced to combat Jewish slander regarding the manner of Jesus' birth." I consider the latter very improbable.

142 There is no known messianic interpretation of this verse in Judaism. Matthew may have been encouraged to quote it because it continues with the son's being called "Emmanuel," which he translates as "God is with us." It should be noted that R. Yose b. Ḥanina, a second generation Palestinian Amora (*Introduction* 96), interprets the אֶת of Exod 2:6 not as a sign of the accusative, but to mean that the Shechinah, the Divine Presence, was "with" (BDB 85) the infant Moses. Cf. *b. Soṭah* 12b (Soncino 63, with n. 6) and *Exod. Rab.* Shemoth 1/24 on Exod 2:6

## Summary

The above analysis of seven similarities between Matthew's description of Joseph's behavior in regard to Mary, the mother of Israel's final redeemer, in 1:18-25, and Palestinian Judaic tradition on Amram's behavior in regard to Jochebed, the mother of Israel's first redeemer, some of them even identical verbally, points to the latter haggadic narrative as the main source from which Matthew borrowed for his portrayal of the marital relationship between Joseph and Mary. The miraculous conception by Jochebed, whom God restored to her youth, including virginity, also served as a model to Matthew, or already to the Jewish Christian community in which he lived, in regard to the miraculous conception and "virgin birth" of Jesus. However, in Palestinian Judaic tradition it is assumed that Jochebed ( like Sarah, the daughters of Zelophehad, and later her own married daughter Miriam) then had intercourse with her husband, again losing her virginity, and bore the first redeemer of Israel, Moses. Only Hellenistic Judaism, as still attested in Philo of Alexandria, maintained that famous Hebrew women such as Sarah conceived virginally from their husband God, without intercourse with their earthly male partners.

Matthew, who lived in a bilingual community of Palestinian and Hellenistic Jewish Christians, appropriated from the latter

---

(Mirqin 5.37-38, Soncino 3.29-30). If this tradition is ultimately early and Matthew knew of it, God's Presence at the infancy of Moses may also have influenced his quoting Isa 7:14. As God was present in a special way during the infancy of the first redeemer of Israel, so He was also present in a special way at the birth of the final redeemer of Israel. Mary's virginal conception of Jesus, without sexual intercourse with Joseph, also meant that later Christians could now think of him as sinless already at his birth. Cf. Ps 5:7 (Eng. 5), as well as *Sifre* Deut Ha'azinu 321 on Deut 32:25 (Finkelstein 370, Hammer 332): "as free from sin as is a virgin who has never tasted sin." Judaic sources, however, only speak of the *adult* Messiah as free from sin. See *Pss. Sol.* 17:36 (*OTP* 2.668), from Jerusalem and the middle of the first century BCE, and originally in Hebrew (R. B. Wright in 2.640-642); *T. Judah* 24:1 (*OTP* 1.801); John 7:18; 8:46; 2 Cor 5:21; Heb 4:15; 7:26; 1 Pet 1:19; 2:22; and 1 John 3:5.

group Mary's remaining a virgin until the birth of Jesus. He artistically combined this, however, with the well-attested Palestinian Judaic motif of the Holy Spirit's "coming upon" Miriam (Aramaic Maryam, Latin Maria), who prophesied that the child her mother was to bear would redeem Israel. Luke 1:34-35 shows that approximately the same phenomenon also took place in the Hellenistic Jewish Christian community from which the Evangelist Luke drew his material in regard to the "virginal conception" of Jesus. The *clear* interweaving of both Palestinian and Hellenistic Judaic materials from the haggadah of Moses' miraculous conception and birth, however, was the major merit of the Evangelist Matthew in his chapters one and two. In this respect he resembles a scribe trained for the kingdom of heaven who brings out of his treasure both what is new and what is already known (13:52).

# VI. Other Parallels to the Virginal Conception from the History of Religions

Scholars have called attention to many other instances of the virginal conception of pagan heroes or very important persons.[142a] To my mind only one is directly relevant to the virginal conception of Jesus.

The Roman historian Suetonius published *The Lives of the Caesars* in 120 CE.[143] In Book II, "The Deified Augustus," he describes in 94.3 how, according to Julius Marathus, a few months before the future emperor was born a portent ( *prodigium* ) was observed at Rome signifying that "nature was pregnant with a king for the Roman people. Thereupon the senate in consternation decreed that no male child born that year should be reared. However, those whose wives were pregnant saw to it that the decree was not filed in the treasury [thus becoming valid], since each one appropriated the prediction to his own family."[144]

This is slightly reminiscent of Pharaoh's decree in Exod 1:22 that all the (male) children of the Hebrews should be killed.

---

[142a] In addition to the works of Eduard Norden, Martin Dibelius and Walter Radl cited in notes 110 and 89, cf. Ernst Nellessen, *Das Kind und seine Mutter* (SBS 39; Stuttgart: Katholisches Bibelwerk, 1969) 100-109; Joachim Gnilka, *Das Matthäusevangelium*. I. Teil (HTKNT 1,1; Freiburg: Herder, 1986) 23-28; and Raymond Brown, *The Birth of the Messiah* 522-523. In addition, Ulrich Luz in *Das Evangelium nach Matthäus*, 1. Teilband, Mt 1-7, p. 144, also calls attention to the Jewish writing 2 (Slavonic) Enoch 71:1-23 (OTP 1.204-207), where Melkisedek's mother bears him in her old age without having slept with her husband, although she is no longer a virgin. At her death the child emerges from her, sits on the side of the bed, as large as a three-year-old, and immediately blesses the Lord. As F. Andersen points out in his notes, "The circumstances of Melchizedek's conception are closer to those of the conception of Mary herself in the Book of James (James, ANT, p. 20)" (204-205). The date of the narrative is also very problematical (94-97). I thus do not share Luz's assertion that it is "very closely related" to Matt 1:18-20.

[143] Cf. LCL I. xii.

[144] I slightly modify the LCL translation of J. Rolfe.

Judaic tradition adds that Pharaoh's advisors told him that he could thus prevent the birth of the future redeemer of Israel.

In 94.4 Suetonius continues by citing an incident from the *Theologumena* of Asclepius of Mendes. Caesar Augustus' mother Atia once attended a service of Apollo in the middle of the night, falling asleep in the temple. A serpent[145] then glided up to her and departed. After awakening, Atia found a mark on her body like a serpent, which could not be removed. Ten months later Augustus was born "and was therefore regarded as the 'son of Apollo' ( *Apollinis filium* )." Before giving birth, Atia had also dreamed that her inner organs were carried up to the stars "and spread over the whole extent of land and sea, while [her husband] Octavius dreamed that the sun rose from Atia's womb."

Caesar Augustus was born in 63 BCE (5), ruled alone for forty-four years (8.3), and died in 14 CE, shortly before he turned seventy-six (100.1). Augustus was to be regarded as the "son of [the god] Apollo" because of the incident described above.[146]

---

145 Cf. Rolfe's note "c" on this, as well as his note "a" on 60. In Plutarch's biography of Alexander the Great, the historian also describes in 2.6 how "a serpent was once seen lying stretched out by the side of (his mother) Olympias as she slept," and in 3.2 his father Philip once beheld the god (Zeus) Ammon "in the form of a serpent, sharing the couch of his wife." Olympias later told her adult son "the secret of his begetting" (3.3). See the LCL translation by Bernadotte Perrin of *Plutarch's Lives*, 7.226-229. Here too Olympias is described as becoming pregnant from a god, yet *after* the consummation of her marriage to Philip. For the Greek tradition of conception via a god in the form of a serpent, see Dieter Zeller, "Geburtsankündigung und Geburtsverkündigung. Formge-schichtliche Untersuchung im Blick auf Mt 1f, Lk 1f" in *Studien und Texte zur Formgeschichte*, ed. Klaus Berger et al. (TANZ 7; Tübingen: Francke Verlag, 1992) 59-134, p. 88 with n. 78.

146 Although Augustus was born ten months after his mother Atia visited the temple of Apollo, Octavius was not presented here as his biological father, as one would first suppose. These were most likely shorter lunar months, equivalent roughly to nine solar months, the normal term of pregnancy. Cf. Wis 7:2 and the quotation from Vergil's *Aeneid*, Eclogue 4, in Hans-Josef Klauck, *The Religious Context of Early Christianity. A Guide to Graeco-Roman Religions* (Edinburgh: Clark, 2000) 288.

Other prodigia indicated that he (as the Roman Emperor) would rule over the entire world, both on land and at sea, indeed, that he would be the center or life-giving source of the universe (the sun).[147]

After his death Augustus was deified (97.1), thus becoming *Divus Augustus*.[148] Yet even during his lifetime he was labeled in Asia Minor "the native Zeus and savior of the human race." An effort was made there for "the birthday of the divine emperor," September 23rd, to be made into New Year's Day.[149]

It is hard to believe that the Evangelist Matthew, also Greek-speaking, was not aware of such developments. When he describes the birth of Jesus as taking place before the death of Herod the Great in 4 BCE (2:1), and thus during the reign of Augustus,[150] he may be intentionally contrasting the birthday of the "king of the Jews" (v 2) with the birthday of the contemporary king-emperor of the entire Roman Empire, celebrated with great pomp. Caesar Augustus, given divine attributes before and after his death, and considered to be the son of the god Apollo already at his birth, for Matthew was also not the true savior of the world, the Son of God. The latter was rather Jesus (27:54), born of a virgin, without her fiancé's / husband's participation (1:18-25).[151]

---

[147] Cf. also the predictions and signs in 94.5-6. A parallel to the above traditions is found in Dio Cassius' *Roman History* 45.1.2-5. It was probably written sometime in the years 200-222 CE (LCL, I. xiii).

[148] Cf. also 97.2 on his being numbered with the gods.

[149] Cf. the texts cited by Klauck in his *The Religious Context of Early Christianity* 296-298, and the entire section on Augustus in 294-301 within the context of "Divinised Human Beings."

[150] Cf. Luke 2:1 for Jesus' birth as explicitly taking place during the reign of the Emperor Augustus.

[151] In the Augustus myth, the god Apollo in the form of a serpent impregnates his mother, already married and no longer a virgin. The Matthean account outdoes this: the "Holy Spirit" comes upon Mary, still a virgin, and she conceives.

## VII. Judaic Allegations of Jesus' Illegitimacy

Judaic assertions of Jesus' illegitimacy are quite vague and late.[152] The following three passages are most relevant.

a)  In the uncensored text of *b. Šabb.* 104b the statement is made: "But his mother was Miriam the hairdresser? – It is as we say in Pumbeditha: 'This one has been unfaithful to her husband.'"[153]

"Miriam" ( מרים ) is correct here for Jesus' mother Mary, yet she has been confused with Mary "Magdalene," similar to "hairdresser." Pumbeditha was the seat of one of the Babylonian academies, now a part of Baghdad in Irak.[154]　The above tradition thus arose in Babylonia and not in Palestine. The verb "has been unfaithful to" is סטת ד אן מ, lit. "to turn from," but meant as "to go astray; to be faithless."[155]

The whole passage is late, probably from the fourth century CE, non-Palestinian, and unintentionally distorts the contents of the Gospels (Mary and Mary Magdalene).

b)  In *b. Sanh.* 106a, R. Papa, a fifth generation Babylonian Amora who was active near Sura on the Euphrates, also now a part of Baghdad, and who died in 375 CE,[156] remarks: "This is

---

[152] For an overview, cf. the classical work by R. Travor Herford, *Christianity in Talmud and Midrash* (London: Williams & Norgate, 1903; reprint New York: KTAV, 1975), especially 35-50. He includes a discussion of Ben Stada and Ben Pandira, which can be consulted on them. See also Raymond Brown, *The Birth of the Messiah* 534-537. The Jews' response to Jesus in John 8:41, "We are not illegitimate children," is not an assertion of *his* illegitimacy, as sometimes thought.　None of the Judaic passages cited below justifies the assertion of Schaberg – followed by others – that Jesus was the result of Mary's being raped (see n. 52).

[153] Soncino 504, with n. 2. A parallel is found in *b. Sanh.* 67a (Soncino 456, with n. 5).

[154] Cf. *Introduction* 4.

[155] Jastrow 972.

[156] *Introduction* 106-107, 4 and 13.

what men say, 'She who was the descendant of princes and governors played the harlot with carpenter(s).'"[157]

R. Papa's assertion that Jesus' mother Mary descended from "princes and governors" may reflect another mixing up of two Miriams, as in a) above. This time Mary (Miriam), the mother of Jesus, could have been given the genealogy of Miriam, Moses' sister, who in Judaic tradition became an ancestor of David (see notes 120 and 121). Or, more plausibly, since Joseph was not considered to be Jesus' father, his genealogy in Matt 1:1-17, including David, "princes and governors," was thought to apply to Mary.[158]

The Munich MS of the Talmud has the singular "carpenter," an allusion to Joseph's profession as described in Matt 13:55.

The verb "played the harlot" is from זנה , זנא : to run about as a prostitute, to be faithless.[159] Here Mary is accused of being unfaithful to her "husband" (Joseph), a "carpenter."

This statement is also Babylonian and thus non-Palestinian, from the fourth century CE, and aware only in a vague way of Gospel traditions.

c) In *Pesiq. R.* 21/6 on "face to face" in Deut 5:4, R. Levi, a third generation Palestinian Amora,[160] notes that Daniel says in 7:9 : "As I watched, thrones were set in place, and an Ancient of Days sat down...."

In *b. Sanh.* 38b, R. Akiba, a second generation Tanna,[161] maintains that one of these thrones is for God and the other for David (the Messiah).[162]

Knowledge of the above messianic interpretation of Dan 7:9 is presupposed in the continuation of *Pesiq. R.* 21/6. R. Ḥiyya

---

[157] Soncino 725.

[158] So Herford in *Christianity in Talmud and Midrash* 48. Cf. also *b. Sanh.* 43a (Soncino 282), where Jesus is stated to be connected to מלכות . The latter could be either the government or royalty (the kingdom of David). See also the additional sources cited in n. 120.

[159] Jastrow 406.

[160] *Introduction* 98.

[161] *Introduction* 79.

[162] Soncino 245, as a baraitha.

bar Abba, also a third generation Palestinian Amora,[163] now states in regard to God's guises: "If a whoreson should say to you, 'There are two different gods,' quote God as saying in reply: 'I am the One of the (Red) Sea and I am the One of Sinai.'"[164]

"A whoreson" here is the Aramaic בְּרָא דְזְנִיתָא , son of a whore or prostitute.[165] Here a Palestinian rabbi definitely refers to Mary as a whore, for in the messianic context of Dan 7:9[166] Jesus is certainly meant by him who maintains there are two different gods, i.e. God the Father and himself as the Son of God.

Although Palestinian, the above discussion is only from the end of the third century CE. It betrays no special knowledge of Mary except to brand her as a whore or prostitute. It too is based on only vague knowledge of Matt 1:18-25.

The above three passages show that while some information regarding Mary's marital relationship to Joseph was known to a number of rabbis, especially in Babylonia, it was garbled and diffuse, late,[167] and only based on the contents of the Gospels

---

163 *Introduction* 99.

164 Friedmann 100b-101a; Braude 422, whom I slightly alter. The rabbi repeats the expression "whoreson" a bit later.

165 Jastrow 406-407 on זְנִיתָא ; it is equivalent to the Hebrew זוֹנָה , harlot (388,2).

166 Cf. the son of man in v 13, and on the messianic interpretation of these verses Str-B 1.485-486. See also Ps 110:1 applied to the Messiah by Jesus in Mark 12:36 par., as well as Acts 2:34-35.

167 The Mishnah passage *Yebam.* 4:13 (Albeck 3.33, Danby 225) is much earlier, but it only very improbably alludes to Jesus. It reads in regard to a *mamzer*, a bastard (Jastrow 794): "R. Simeon b. Azzai (a second generation Tanna: *Introduction* 82) said: 'I found a family register in Jerusalem and in it was written, Such-a-one is a bastard through [a transgression of the law of] thy neighbor's wife (Lev 18:20)....'" A מַמְזֵר is one of "those born of an illicit union" in Deut 23:2. While the term "such-a-one" ( פְּלוֹנִי ) may elsewhere allude to Jesus in Judaic sources, here it does not since Lev 18:20 does not refer to adultery, but to incest with a "kinsman's" wife. Mary and Joseph, however, were not related to each other. Secondly, their "family register" would not have been stored in the archives of far-off Jerusalem, and this "register"

themselves, especially Matt 1:18-25. It is thus of no relevance to the question of the origin of Mary's virginal conception.

---

should not be equated with the beginning of Matthew's Gospel (against Herford, *Christianity in Talmud and Midrash* 45). Bruce Chilton thinks Joseph still lived in the site Bethlehem "of Galilee" when Mary became pregnant from him in Nazareth. She then gave birth to Jesus in this Bethlehem to prevent rumors. Joseph later moved with Mary and Jesus to Nazareth. Thus Jesus was considered a *mamzer* in Nazareth and suffered his entire life from the ostracism caused by this phenomenon. See his *Rabbi Jesus. An Intimate Biography* (New York: Doubleday, 2000), chapter one, "A *Mamzer* from Nazareth" (pp. 3-22), as well as his art. "Jésus, le *mamzer* (Mt 1.18)" in *NTS* 47 (2001) 222-227. Chilton's very imaginative theory is unnecessary in light of the explanation of Mary's virginal conception I propose above. On this topic see now also Scot McKnight, "Calling Jesus *Mamzer*," in the *Journal for the Study of the Historical Jesus* 1 (2003) 73-103.

# VIII. Haggadah and the Historicity
## of the Virginal Conception

"Haggadah" ( הַגָּדָה )[168] or "aggadah" ( אַגָּדָה or אֲגָדָה )[169] is usually defined negatively as the opposite of legal or *halakhic* interpretation.[170] It includes wordplays, free associations, exaggerations and "imaginative dramatization."[171] One sub-category of narrative haggadah is the miracle narrative.[172] The Judaic account of Amram's divorcing and re-marrying Jochebed, based primarily on haggadic interpretation of Exod 2:1,[173] is an excellent example of such a miracle narrative. When Amram takes Jochebed back, a "miracle" occurs and God restores the status of youth to her, including her virginity.

Did those who created the latter narrative, whether in the synagogue or the study house (beth ha-midrash) or in both, expect their hearers to believe in its historicity? The question itself would have seemed strange to them. As Chronicles supplemented the Books of Kings, filling in gaps by adding names and concrete details, so the haggadic method of interpretation continued for centuries after the closure of the Hebrew Bible, especially the Pentateuch, in Palestine. The biblical narrative of Moses' birth was commented on and filled out not only in the LXX and the various targums, but also in the midrashim and other sources cited in the Introduction. The added details, such as Jochebed's return to the status of youth, including virginity, were felt to be "true" in a religious sense.

---

168 Jastrow 330.
169 Jastrow 11.
170 Cf. the art. "Aggadah" in *EJ* (1971) 2.354-364, and Stemberger, *Introduction* 58, 259-261, and 39 (calling attention to Palestinian books or collections of haggadah already in the third century CE).
171 Cf. Judah Goldin, *The Song at the Sea* (Philadelphia and New York: The Jewish Publication Society, 1990; original New Haven: Yale University Press, 1971) 27 in his chapter "5. Haggadic Interpretation."
172 Stemberger, *Introduction* 58.
173 Cf. *m. 'Abot* 5:22 (Albeck 4.381, Danby 458), where Ben Bag-Bag says: "Turn it (the Torah) and turn it again, for everything is in it." This could be applied to individual verses such as Exod 2:1.

They were developed via "the poetic license of every creative story-teller"[174] in part in order to encourage those who were in a difficult situation to recall how God had rescued the Israelites in dire straits in Egypt. He thus restored Jochebed's youth to her, including virginity, so that she could bear the first redeemer of Israel, Moses. These were thus in part words of consolation: As God then helped His people in Egypt in a miraculous way, so He now can miraculously help you too in your present situation.

Secondly, haggadic amplifications such as Amram's being the head of the Sanhedrin in Egypt, with an emphasis on his "righteousness," were designed in part to provide role models for the narrators' hearers. By experiencing how he acted "righteously" when taking back his wife Jochebed, the hearers themselves were encouraged to act just as "righteously" when in a similarly difficult situation.

Thirdly, and more importantly, God's miraculously restoring Jochebed to her youth, including virginity, is a part of the overall glorification of Moses, Israel's greatest hero, starting already with his birth. Such glorification, which also took place outside Israel (cf. for example the miraculous conception of Caesar Augustus in section VI. above), was standard haggadic practice in regard to Israel's greatest personages. First-century Jews in Palestine would even have considered it strange if their illustrious lawgiver had *not* been greatly extolled, including at his birth. They did not ask the question of whether haggadic embellishments were historically "true." By its conveying moral and ethical principles, haggadah according to Moshe David Herr, however, "does contain truth which is greater than that of historical and philological reality, and more important than that of the natural sciences." "The fact that in this topic there is no place for rational and unambiguous decisions does not diminish its importance."[175]

---

[174] Cf. the art. "Aggadah" in *EJ* (1971) 2. 354. Embellishment, of course, also aided in satisfying popular curiosity in regard to what was not openly stated in the biblical text.

[175] *Ibid.*, 355. On p. 356 he notes *b. Yoma* 75a (Soncino 362), which states that haggadah "draws the heart of man," i.e. it touches one's emotions.

I proposed above that the bilingual Jewish Christian Matthew derived most of the motifs and terminology in 1:18-25 from his own Semitic-speaking Jewish Christian community, where the haggadic narrative of Moses' birth was greatly cherished and retold again and again. This included God's miraculously restoring Jochebed to her youth, including virginity, so that she could bear the first redeemer of Israel, Moses, to her husband Amram (after having had sexual union with him). Hellenistic Jewish Christians from the same Matthean community provided him with the further embellishment of this motif still known to us from the writings of Philo of Alexandria. The latter notes for example that God restored the matriarch Sarah to her virginity, and she then bore Isaac to Abraham without first having sexual union with him. Indeed, God was allegorically her "husband." These Hellenistic Jewish Christians, certainly also well acquainted with God's miraculously restoring Jochebed to her youth, including virginity, then added the further Hellenistic Jewish embellishment of this motif, virginal conception, to Mary the mother of Israel's final redeemer, the Messiah. It was from this final stage within his own bilingual community that the Evangelist Matthew borrowed the motif.[176]

While no absolute certainty can be obtained in this matter, I doubt very much whether Philo himself actually believed that Sarah conceived Isaac as a virgin, without intercourse with Abraham. Neither the Hellenistic Jewish Christians of Matthew's community who applied this motif to Mary considered it "factual," nor did the Evangelist.[177] They were too well

---

[176] The same was true for the Evangelist Luke. He inherited or borrowed the motif of the virginal conception from his own Hellenistic Jewish Christian community.

[177] Against for example Raymond Brown in *The Birth of the Messiah* 517 and 704-705, who includes the Evangelist Luke. Brown simply does not appreciate the nature of Judaic haggadah. Cf. also Luz, *Das Evangelium nach Matthäus* 1.155. In his revised dissertation on the Matthean and Lukan birth narratives, *Midrash Criticism. Introduction and Appraisal* (Lanham, MD: University Press of America, 1998), Charles Quarles maintains that these Evangelists did not develop "theological tales," which are "fiction," as haggadah is "fable," "Jewish myth" ( *passim* ). Although he grants that "creative historiography" is found in the

acquainted with the embellishing nature of haggadah to do so.[178] Matthew, for example, never again refers to the motif in his entire Gospel. Passages such as 12:46-50 and 13:54-58 show no acquaintance with it. Rather, Mary's virginal conception of Jesus was intended to show that, as in Judaic haggadic tradition on the birth of Moses, it is God Himself who is miraculously at work here. It is His Spirit, the Holy Spirit, who enables Mary to bear the redeemer / savior of Israel. Although Jesus is thus not called God's Son *expressis verbis* here,[179] he is shown to be so. The beginning of the Gospel thus corresponds to its end, where the pagan centurion and those with him who watch over Jesus on the Cross say: "Truly this man was God's Son!" (27:54).

---

Protevangelium of James, this is definitely not true for Matthew and Luke, who did not intend to "deceive" their readers. Concerned with "biblical inerrancy" (p. xiii), Quarles feels threatened by what he considers "The Erosion of the Historical Foundations of the Christian Faith" (p. 93). He unfortunately does not comprehend the nature of haggadah, nor does he recognize how parts of the early Judaic midrash on Exodus 1-2 regarding Moses' birth (still found for example in *b. Sotah* and *Exodus Rabbah* ) provided part of the background to Matthew's own narrative of Jesus' birth.

[178] In *b. Sotah* 12a on Exod 2:2 (Soncino 61) and *Exod. Rab.* Shemoth 1/20 on the same verse (Mirqin 5.34, with other parallels in n. 3; Soncino 3.27), as well as Pseudo-Philo 9:13 (*OTP* 2.316), it is maintained for example that Moses was born circumcised. According to my wife, a pediatrician, this can indeed happen, but only extremely rarely (*hypospadias* in an advanced form). The first hearers of this haggadah did not ask whether Moses' being born circumcised was factually, biologically true. Rather, they understood its original intention to glorify Moses, the future redeemer of Israel, at his birth. He was already then someone very special. In his *Messias und Gottessohn. Herkunft und Sinn der matthäischen Geburts- und Kindheitsgeschichte* (Düsseldorf: Patmos, 1971) 30, Anton Vögtle incorrectly maintains that the infancy haggadoth of Moses and other great Israelites in Jewish opinion were a part of (God's) "revealed word." That is only true of the oral Torah, also thought to have been revealed to Moses at Sinai, and not of haggadah in general.

[179] Cf. also "God is with us" in 1:23 and the citation of Hos 11:1 in 2:15.

Was Mary's miraculous virginal conception of Jesus "historical"? No. Yet as a typically Jewish Christian haggadic embellishment of the birth of Israel's final redeemer, the Messiah, it conveys a "religious truth," that Jesus already at his birth was the Son of God. It is one of the tragedies of the Christian church that the number of its Palestinian Jewish members dwindled so rapidly after the very successful missionizing of Gentiles. The latter soon made them into sects such as the Palestinian Ebionites, who went so far as to deny the virginal conception of Jesus by making his sonship begin with his baptism.[180] As Palestinians, they could not accept the Hellenistic Jewish Christian further embellishment of the basically Palestinian haggadic motif of God's restoring Jochebed to a state of youth, including virginity, by then applying this to Jesus as being conceived even without a human father.

Early Palestinian and Hellenistic Jewish Christians could have conveyed to Gentile Christians the nature of Judaic haggadah, and the centuries-old Gentile Christian debate in regard to the "historicity" or "facticity" of Mary's virginal conception of Jesus would have been unnecessary. Mary was certainly a virgin when Joseph became engaged to and married her, only then having intercourse with her. In spite of her not actually conceiving Jesus as a virgin, Christians today can rightly revere Mary as the young Jewish woman whom God chose to bear His Son, the Messiah or final redeemer of Israel, just as contemporary Jews can rightly revere Jochebed, whom God chose to bear the first redeemer of Israel, Moses.

---

[180] Cf. Schneemelcher, *New Testament Apocrypha* 1.168, as well as Irenaeus, *Against Heresies* I. 26.1-2; III. 11.7 and 21.1, the latter dealing with Isa 7:14 (*The Ante-Nicene Fathers* 1.352, 428 and 451, with 312 for the work being written between 182-188 CE), and Eusebius, *Eccl. Hist.* VI. 17 (LCL II. 50-51). See also the statement by Trypho the Jew in Justin Martyr's *Dialogue with Trypho* 49:1 : "we all expect that Christ will be a man [born] of men..." (Marcovich 150; *The Ante-Nicene Fathers* 1.219).

# An Ecumenical Epilogue

As shown above, both Palestinian and Hellenistic Judaic haggadic traditions regarding Jochebed, Amram, Miriam and the birth of Moses developed at a very early time and strongly influenced Matthew's portrayal of Mary and Joseph and the birth of Jesus in 1:18–2:23. It is not at all surprising that the same type of haggadic embellishment continued in early Christian communities in regard to the "holy family." So-called "Infancy Gospels" arose, which combined materials from the birth narratives of Matthew and Luke with further legendary elements.[1]

The most important and influential infancy gospel was the "Protevangelium of James."[2] Probably from the second half of the second century CE, it has survived in many MSS and versions, showing its great popularity.[3] For the first time Mary's

---

[1] Cf. Oscar Cullmann's section "X. Infancy Gospels" in Wilhelm Schneemelcher's *New Testament Apocrypha* 1.414-469.

[2] *Ibid.*, 1.421-439.

[3] *Ibid.*, 1.421-424. Cullmann thinks its author cannot have been a Jewish Christian because of his lack of knowledge of Palestine's geography and Jewish customs. Yet the "Judaea" of 21:1 and 4 (pp. 435-436) was probably changed from "Jerusalem" (in 20:3) by an earlier copiest; Mary's upbringing in the Jerusalem Temple is patently based on the child Samuel's upbringing in the Temple (of Shiloh) in 1 Samuel 1-3; and the author's language is steeped in the OT (see the numerous references on pp. 437-439). Notes on Judaic haggadic traditions could be added, especially in regard to the child Samuel. See my "The Child Jesus in the Temple (Luke 2:41-51a), and Judaic Traditions on the Child Samuel in the Temple (1 Samuel 1-3)" in *Samuel, Saul and Jesus* 1-64. A "Samuel" is even mentioned in 10:2 and 17:2. The healing of Salome's hand by touching the infant Jesus (20:3) is based on the Egyptian princess's being healed of leprosy immediately after she touches the infant Moses.

parents Joachim and Anna are mentioned by name (1:1-2 and elsewhere); Joseph is portrayed as an elderly widower with older sons (9:2 and elsewhere, in contrast to Mark 6:3 par.); Mary is herself of Davidic descent (10:1); her virginity and Joseph's not touching her before the birth of Jesus are greatly emphasized (10-16); and Mary's virginity also *after* giving birth, i.e. her perpetual virginity, is even attested physically (19:3 – 20:1).[4]

Oscar Cullmann correctly observes that "devotion to Mary had already made considerable advances even at the comparatively early date when the book was written," and that the Protevangelium "had a powerful influence on the development of Mariology."[5] Its great effect on literature and art

---

[4] Salome states in 19:3, "As the Lord my God lives, *unless I put (forward) my finger* and test her condition, *I will not believe* that a virgin has brought forth" (*New Testament Apocrypha* 1.434). As Cullmann in part points out, the italicized imagery derives from John 20:25 in regard to doubting Thomas. Cf. also *Mart. Isa.* 11 for Mary as "of the family of David the prophet" (v 2); her miraculous birth of Jesus (v 8); and her womb then being in the same (virginal) status as before her conceiving (v 9; *OTP* 2.174-175). Michael Knibb believes that the Vision of Isaiah, of which this is a part, ultimately goes back to the second century CE (2.150). Enrico Norelli in "Avant le canonique et l'apocryphe: aux récits de la naissance de Jésus " in *RTP* 126 (1994) 305-324 proposes that there was a *testimonium* regarding the virginal conception already in the first century which influenced *Mart. Isa.* 11 and *Acts of Peter* 24; it was not dependent on the Matthean or Lukan nativity narratives. The motif was connected with the Davidic origin of the Messiah and functioned as anti-Jewish polemic (p. 320). Norelli is not aware here of Judaic Moses traditions.

[5] *New Testament Apocrypha* 1.425. Cf. also the discussion in John N. D. Kelly, *Early Christian Doctrines* (London and New York: Continuum, 2003[5]) 492-493, with a survey of the development of Marian veneration on pp. 493-499. See also Stephen Benko, *The Virgin Goddess.* Studies in the Pagan and Christian Roots of Mariology (Studies in the History of Religions 59; Leiden: Brill, 1993) 196-202, and his last two chapters, "From Devotion to Doctrine" and "Mary and the History of Salvation." Benko demonstrates the great role popular piety played in the development of Mariology, which "offers a way to deal with a major

up to the period of the Reformation was primarily due to the fact that parts of it were incorporated into the Latin "Gospel of Pseudo-Matthew," which became very popular.[6]

Within the Christian Church, both Eastern and Western, the figure of Mary continued to be embellished throughout the centuries, primarily due to popular piety. The Council of Ephesus in 431 CE furthered the dissemination of the term *theotokos* ( θεοτόκος ), "God-bearer," for Mary. The Second Council of Constantinople in 553 noted her perpetual virginity ( ἀειπάρθενος ),[7] as already expressed in the Protevangelium of James (see above). The Second Council of Nicea in 787 spoke of her as "our lord" ( δέσποινα ἡμῶν ). Within the last 150 years Pope Pius IX. on December 8, 1854 decreed that all the faithful should believe that Mary remained pure of original sin, i.e. her own conception by Anna was immaculate (the *immaculata conceptio* ), and on November 1, 1950 Pope Pius XII. declared the dogma that Mary at her death was not buried on earth, but ascended directly to heaven ( her *assumptio* ), to be celebrated annually on August 15th.[8]

Of the numerous Marian festivals, North American Lutherans for example have retained February 2nd as "the

---

deficiency of Christian theology in which the feminine image of God has all but disappeared" (p. 265).

[6] *New Testament Apocrypha* 1.418-419.

[7] For the term, cf. already Philo in *Cong.* 7 on Sarah.

[8] Cf. the Catholic Dormitio Church in Jerusalem. Nevertheless, Mary's tomb is revered at two sites. Just north of the present Garden of Gethsemane at the base of the Mount of Olives she is supposedly interred, with her parents Joachim and Anna, as well as Joseph, elsewhere in the same sanctuary (Vilnay, *Israel Guide* 155). Another tradition maintains Jesus' favorite disciple John took her along to Ephesus, where her tomb is displayed and also visited by Moslems. See Selahattin Erdemgil, *Ephesos* (Istanbul: Net Turistik Yayinlar, 1989) 118-120. In his exhaustive study *Ancient Traditions of the Virgin Mary's Dormition and Assumption* (Oxford Early Christian Studies; Oxford: Oxford University Press, 2002), Stephen Shoemaker states: "Despite years of research, the historical record has still yielded no clear witness to the Virgin's Dormition and Assumption from the earliest church" (p. 10; see also p. 13). Only in the seventh century CE did the Dormition begin to be located on Mount Zion (p. 106).

presentation of our Lord," March 25th as "the annunciation of our Lord," May 31st as "the visitation," and August 15th as a special day commemorating "Mary, mother of our Lord."[9] German Protestants celebrate only the first three on February 2nd, March 25th and July 2nd.[10]

It is encouraging that major Lutheran and Roman Catholic theologians in North America can emphasize the "church-uniting convergences" in regard to the role of Mary,[11] although the Roman Catholic dogmas proclaimed in 1854 and 1950 still present major hindrances to ecumenical dialogue in this regard.[12]     Nevertheless, after a long period of radical oversensitivity to the figure of Mary beginning with the sixteenth-century Reformation, Protestants too have begun to appreciate Mary more and more as a very positive model of faith.[13]

It is my modest hope that the above exegetical study of Matt 1:18 – 2:23, including an explanation of the Palestinian and

---

[9] Cf. the *Lutheran Book of Worship* (Minneapolis: Augsburg, 1978) 10-11 and the relevant prayers and readings on pp. 32-33.

[10] Cf. the *Evangelisches Gottesdienstbuch* (Berlin: Verlagsgemeinschaft "Evangelisches Gottesdienstbuch," 1999) 424-427 and 432-433. Since the Second Vatican Council, the Roman Catholic Church has no longer celebrated February 2nd and March 25th as Marian, but as festivals of the Lord. In addition, September 8th commemorates Mary's birth, and December 8th / 9th her conception by Anna. On a recent assessment of the veneration of Mary as well as Mariology, see the articles "Marienfeste" and "Marienverehrung" in *RGG*[4] (2002) 5.819-824 and 825-830 by various authors, as well as "Maria / Mariafrömmigkeit" in *TRE* (1992) 22.115-161.

[11] Cf. *The One Mediator, the Saints, and Mary.* Lutherans and Catholics in Dialogue VIII, ed. H. George Anderson, J. Francis Stafford and Joseph A. Burgess (Minneapolis: Augsburg, 1992). A predecessor volume was *Mary in the New Testament*, ed. Raymond E. Brown, Karl P. Donfried, Joseph A. Fitzmyer and John Reumann (Philadelphia: Fortress Press; New York: Paulist Press, 1978).

[12] The Orthodox Church also does not recognize the latter two dogmas.

[13] Cf. for example Beverly Gaventa, *Mary. Glimpses of the Mother of Jesus* (Minneapolis: Fortress, 1999), and the essay volume edited by her and Cynthia Rigby, *Blessed One. Protestant Perspectives on Mary* (Louisville, KY / London: Westminster John Knox, 2002).

Hellenistic Jewish Christian origin of Mary's "virginal conception" of Jesus, may lead to a better understanding of Mary's role in the New Testament and in Christian faith. It can also show contemporary Jews how haggadic Judaic traditions greatly influenced the development of early Christianity through the mediation of Palestinian and Hellenistic Jewish Christians.

# Sources and Reference Works

## I. The Bible

Kittel, *Biblia Hebraica*, ed. R. Kittel et al. (Stuttgart: Privilegierte Württembergische Bibelanstalt, 1951⁷).

Rahlfs, *Septuaginta*, ed. A. Rahlfs (Stuttgart: Württembergische Bibelanstalt, 1962⁷).

Hatch-Redpath, *A Concordance to the Septuagint*, ed. E. Hatch and H. Redpath (Oxford: Clarendon, 1897; corrected reprint Grand Rapids, Michigan: Baker Book House, 1983), 2 volumes.

Nestle / Aland, *Novum Testamentum Graece*, ed. E. Nestle, K. Aland, et al. (Stuttgart: Deutsche Bibelgesellschaft, 1990²⁶).

*The Greek New Testament*, ed. K. Aland, M. Black, B. Metzger and A. Wikgren (London: United Bible Societies, 1966).

*Hebrew New Testament*, by F. Delitzsch (Berlin: Trowitzsch and Son, 1885).

*Hebrew New Testament* (Jerusalem: The United Bible Societies, 1979).

## II. The Targums

Sperber, *The Bible in Aramaic*, ed. A. Sperber (Leiden: Brill, 1959), 4 volumes.

McNamara, *Targum Neofiti 1: Genesis*, trans. M. McNamara (The Aramaic Bible, 1A; Edinburgh: Clark, 1992).

Maher, *Targum Pseudo-Jonathan: Genesis*, trans. M. Maher (The Aramaic Bible, 1B; Edinburgh: Clark, 1992). *Exodus*, 1994.

Drazin, *Targum Onkelos to Exodus*, ed. and trans. I. Drazin (New York: Ktav; Denver: Center for Judaic Studies, University of Denver, 1990).

Grossfeld, *The Targum Onqelos to Exodus*, trans. B. Grossfeld (The Aramaic Bible, 7; Edinburgh: Clark, 1988).

McNamara / Maher, *Targum Neofiti 1: Exodus, Targum Pseudo-Jonathan: Exodus*, trans. M. McNamara and M. Maher (The Aramaic Bible, 2; Edinburgh: Clark, 1994).

Clarke, *Targum Pseudo-Jonathan: Numbers*, trans. Ernest Clarke (The Aramaic Bible, 4; Edinburgh: Clark, 1995). Including *Targum Neofiti 1: Numbers*, trans. Martin McNamara.

Rieder, *Targum Jonathan ben Uziel on the Pentateuch*, ed. with a Hebrew translation by D. Rieder (Jerusalem, 1984), 2 volumes.

Díez Macho, *Neophyti 1*, ed. A. Díez Macho (Madrid: Consejo Superior de Investigaciones Científicas, 1968-1978), 5 volumes.

Klein, *The Fragment-Targums of the Pentateuch*, ed. and trans. M. Klein (AnBib 76; Rome: Biblical Institute, 1980), 2 volumes.

Tal, *The Samaritan Targum of the Pentateuch. A Critical Edition*, ed. Abraham Tal, Part I, Genesis, Exodus (Tel-Aviv: Tel-Aviv University, 1980).

## III. The Mishnah and Tosefta

Albeck, *Shisha Sidre Mishna*, ed. Ch. Albeck (Jerusalem and Tel Aviv: Bialik Institute and Dvir, 1975), 6 volumes.

Danby, *The Mishnah*, trans. H. Danby  (London: Oxford University, 1933).

Neusner, *The Mishnah*, trans. J. Neusner  (New Haven: Yale University, 1988).

Zuckermandel, *Tosephta*, ed. M. Zuckermandel, with a supplement by S. Liebermann (Jerusalem: Wahrmann, 1970).

Neusner, *The Tosefta*, trans. J. Neusner et al. (Hoboken, New Jersey: KTAV, 1977-1986), 6 volumes.

## IV. The Talmuds

Soncino, *The Babylonian Talmud*, ed. I. Epstein, various translators (London: Soncino, 1952), 18 volumes and index.

Goldschmidt, *Der Babylonische Talmud,* ed. with a German translation by L. Goldschmidt (Haag: Nijoff, 1933), 9 volumes.

Krotoshin, *Talmud Yerushalmi,* Krotoshin edition (Jerusalem: Shilah, 1969).

Neusner, *The Talmud of the Land of Israel,* trans. J. Neusner et al. (Chicago: University of Chicago, 1982-1995), 34 volumes.

## V. Halakhic Midrashim

Lauterbach, *Mekilta de-Rabbi Ishmael,* ed. and trans. J. Lauterbach (Philadelphia: The Jewish Publication Society of America, 1976), 3 volumes.

Epstein and Melamed, *Mekhilta d'Rabbi Šimʻon b. Jochai,* ed. J. Epstein and E. Melamed (Jerusalem: Hillel Press, 1955; reprint 1979).

Horowitz, *Siphre ad Numeros adjecto Siphre zutta,* ed. H. Horowitz (Jerusalem: Wahrmann, 1976).

Neusner, *Sifre to Numbers,* trans. J. Neusner (BJS 118-119; Atlanta: Scholars Press, 1986), 2 volumes.

Finkelstein, *Sifre on Deuteronomy,* ed. L. Finkelstein (New York: The Jewish Theological Seminary of America, 1969).

Hammer, *Sifre.* A Tannaitic Commentary on the Book of Deuteronomy, trans. R. Hammer (YJS 24; New Haven: Yale University, 1986).

Neusner, *Sifre to Deuteronomy.* An Analytical Translation, trans. J. Neusner (BJS 98 and 101; Atlanta: Scholars Press, 1987), 2 volumes.

## VI. Haggadic Midrashim

Soncino, *Midrash Rabbah,* ed. H. Freedman and M. Simon (London: Soncino, 1939), 9 volumes and index.

*Midrash Rabbah* (Vilna: Romm, 1887).

Mirqin, *Midrash Rabbah,* Pentateuch. Ed. and vocalized by M. Mirqin (Tel Aviv: Yavneh, 1981), 11 volumes.

Theodor and Albeck, *Midrash Bereshit Rabba,* ed. J. Theodor and Ch. Albeck (Jerusalem: Wahrmann, 1965), 3 volumes.

Donsqi, *Midrash Rabbah.   Shir ha-Shirim*, ed. S. Donsqi (Jerusalem: Dvir, 1980).

*Midrash Tanḥuma*, Eshkol edition (Jerusalem: Eshkol, no date).

Berman, *Midrash Tanḥuma-Yelammedenu*, Genesis and Exodus, trans. Samuel Berman (Hoboken, NJ: KTAV Publishing House, 1996).

Buber, *Midrash Tanḥuma*: Ein agadischer Commentar zum Pentateuch, ed. S. Buber (Vilna: Romm, 1885).

Townsend, *Midrash Tanḥuma*, S. Buber Recension, Genesis, trans. John Townsend (Hoboken, NJ: KTAV Publishing House, 1989).

Townsend, *Midrash Tanḥuma*, S. Buber Recension, Exodus and Leviticus, trans. John Townsend (Hoboken, NJ: KTAV Publishing House, 1997).

Bietenhard, *Midrasch Tanḥuma B*, German by H. Bietenhard (Judaica et Christiana 5-6;  Bern: Peter Lang, 1980-1982), 2 volumes.

Mandelbaum, *Pesikta de Rav Kahana*, ed. B. Mandelbaum (New York: The Jewish Theological Seminary of America, 1962), 2 volumes.

Braude and Kapstein, *Pesikta de-Rab Kahana*, trans. W. Braude and I. Kapstein (Philadelphia: The Jewish Publication Society of America, 1975).

Neusner, *Pesiqta de Rab Kahana. An Analytical Translation*, trans. J. Neusner (BJS 122-123;  Atlanta: Scholars Press, 1987).

Friedmann, *Pesikta Rabbati*, ed. M. Friedmann  (Vienna, 1880; reprint Tel Aviv, 1962-1963).

Braude, *Pesikta Rabbati*, trans. W. Braude (YJS 18;  New Haven: Yale University, 1968), 2 volumes.

Friedmann, *Seder Eliahu rabba und Seder Eliahu zuta*, ed. M. Friedmann (Vienna, 1902-1904; reprint Jerusalem, 1969).

Braude and Kapstein, *Tanna debe Eliyyahu*, trans. W. Braude and I. Kapstein (Philadelphia: The Jewish Publication Society of America, 1981).

Buber, *Midrasch Tehillim*, ed. S. Buber (Vilna: Romm, 1891).

Braude, *The Midrash on Psalms*, trans. W. Braude (YJS 13, 1-2; New Haven: Yale University, 1959), 2 volumes.

Buber, *Midrasch Mischle*, ed. S. Buber (Vilna, 1893; reprint Jerusalem, 1965).

Visotzky, *The Midrash on Proverbs*, trans. B. Visotzky (YJS 27; New Haven: Yale University, 1992).

Wünsche, "Der Midrasch Sprüche," German by A. Wünsche in *Bibliotheca Rabbinica* (Leipzig: Schulze, 1885) 4.1-77.

Eshkol, *Pirqe Rabbi Eliezer*, Eshkol edition (Jerusalem: Eshkol, 1973).

Friedlander, *Pirke de Rabbi Eliezer*, trans. G. Friedlander (New York: Hermon, 1970; original London, 1916).

Buber, *Midrasch Suta*, ed. S. Buber (Berlin: Mekize Nirdamim, 1894).

Buber, *Midrash Sekhel Tob*, ed. S. Buber (Berlin, 1900/1901).

Guggenheimer, *Seder Olam*. The Rabbinic View of Biblical Chronology, trans. Heinrich Guggenheimer (Northvale, NJ, and Jerusalem: Jason Aronson, 1998).

Goldschmidt, *Sefer hajaschar*, ed. Lazarus Goldschmidt (Berlin: Benjamin Harz, 1923).

Noach, *The Book of Jashar*, trans. M. Noach (New York, 1840; reprint Salt Lake City: J. H. Parry, 1887).

Gaster, *The Chronicles of Jerahmeel*, trans. Moses Gaster, prolegomenon by Haim Schwarzbaum (New York: KTAV Publishing House, 1971).

Jellinek, *Bet ha-Midrasch*, ed. A. Jellinek (Jerusalem: Wahrmann Books, 1967³), 6 volumes in 2.

Wünsche, *Aus Israels Lehrhallen*. German by A. Wünsche (Leipzig: Pfeiffer, 1907–1909; reprint Hildesheim: Olms, 1967), 5 volumes.

Margalioth, *Sefer ha-Zohar*, ed. M. Margalioth (Jerusalem: Mossad Harav Kook, 1964), Exodus.

*The Zohar*, trans. H. Sperling, M. Simon and P. Levertoff, 5 volumes (London: Soncino, 1933 / 1956), Vol. III, Shemoth.

\*   \*   \*

Miller, *Molad Mosheh*. Samaritan and Arabic Texts, ed. and trans. Selig J. Miller (New York: Philosophical Library, 1949).

Gaster, *The Asatir*, ed. and trans. Moses Gaster (London: Royal Asiatic Society, 1927).

## VII.  Apocrypha, Pseudepigrapha, Hellenistic Jewish Authors, Philo, Josephus and the Dead Sea Scrolls

Apocrypha:  see Rahlfs, *Septuaginta*.

*OTP. The Old Testament Pseudepigrapha*, ed. J. Charlesworth (Garden City, New York: Doubleday, 1983-1985), 2 volumes.

Charles, *The Greek Versions of the Testaments of the Twelve Patriarchs*, ed. R. H. Charles (Oxford: Clarendon Press, 1908).

Harrington, *Les Antiquités Bibliques*, ed. D. Harrington, French by J. Cazeaux (SC 229-230; Paris: du Cerf, 1976), 2 volumes.

Holladay, *Fragments from Hellenistic Jewish Authors*, Volume II, Poets, ed. and trans. Carl Holladay (Texts and Translations 30, Pseudepigrapha Series 12; Atlanta: Scholars Press, 1989).

LCL, *Philo*, Greek and English translation by F. Colson, G. Whitaker, J. Earp and R. Marcus (Cambridge, MA: Harvard University, 1971), 10 volumes with 2 supplements.

LCL, *Josephus*, Greek and English translation by H. Thackeray, R. Marcus and A. Wikgren (Cambridge, MA: Harvard University, 1969), 9 volumes.

*The Complete Concordance to Flavius Josephus*, Study Edition, ed. Karl Heinrich Rengstorf (Leiden: Brill, 2002), 2 vols., including the *Namenwörterbuch zu Flavius Josephus* by Abraham Schalit.

Martínez and Tigchelaar, *The Dead Sea Scrolls Study Edition*, ed. and trans. F. Martínez and E. Tigchelaar (Leiden: Brill, 2000), 2 volumes.

Charlesworth, *Graphic Concordance to the Dead Sea Scrolls*, ed. J. Charlesworth et al. (Tübingen: Mohr; Louisville: Westminster, John Knox, 1991).

## VIII.  The Early Church, the Koran, and Pagan Authors

Schneemelcher, *New Testament Apocrypha*. Volume One: Gospels and Related Writings, ed. Wilhelm Schneemelcher (Louisville, KY: Westminster / John Knox Press, 1991).

Lake, *The Apostolic Fathers*, trans. Kirsopp Lake (LCL; Cambridge, MA: Harvard University Press, 1912 / 1959), 2 vols.

Marcovich, *Iustini Martyris Dialogus cum Tryphone*, ed. Miroslav Marcovich (Patristische Texte und Studien 47; Berlin: de Gruyter, 1997).

*The Ante-Nicene Fathers*, ed. and trans. Alexander Roberts and James Donaldson, with A. Cleveland Coxe (Grand Rapids, MI: Eerdmans, 1979), vol. I.

Eusebius, *Ecclesiastical History*, trans. J. Oulton (LCL; Cambridge, MA: Harvard University Press, 1932/1973), vol. II.

Pickthall, *The Meaning of the Glorious Koran*, trans. Marmaduke Pickthall (New York: The New American Library of World Literature, 1960).

Suetonius, *The Lives of the Caesars*, trans. J. Rolfe (LCL; Cambridge, MA: Harvard University Press, 1913 / 1989), vol. I.

Dio Cassius, *Dio's Roman History*, Vol. IV, trans. Earnest Carey (LCL; Cambridge, MA: Harvard University Press, 1916 / 1954).

Perrin, *Plutarch's Lives*, Vol. VII, trans. Bernadotte Perrin (LCL; Cambridge, MA: Harvard University Press, 1919 / 1986).

## IX. Dictionaries and Reference Works

BDB, *A Hebrew and English Lexicon of the Old Testament*, by F. Brown, S. Driver and C. Briggs (Oxford: Clarendon, 1962).

Jastrow, *A Dictionary of the Targumim, the Talmud Babli and Yerushalmi, and the Midrashic Literature*, by M. Jastrow (New York: Pardes, 1950), 2 volumes.

Krauss, *Griechische und Lateinische Lehnwörter in Talmud, Midrasch und Targum*, by S. Krauss (Berlin: Calvary, 1898–1899).

Hyman, *Torah Hakethubah Vehamessurah*. A Reference Book of the Scriptural Passages Quoted in Talmudic, Midrashic and Early Rabbinic Literature, by Aaron Hyman, second edition by Arthur Hyman (Tel Aviv: Dvir, 1979), 3 volumes.

Kasher, *Torah Shelemah*, ed. Menachem M. Kasher, vol. VIII, Exodus, Shemoth (New York: American Biblical Encyclopedic Society, 1954²).

Kasher, *Encyclopedia of Biblical Interpretation*, ed. Menachem M. Kasher, vol. VII, Exodus (New York: American Biblical Encyclopedia Society, 1967).

Ginzberg, *The Legends of the Jews*, by L. Ginzberg (Philadelphia: The Jewish Publication Society of America, 1968), 6 volumes and index.

JE, *The Jewish Encyclopedia* (New York: Funk and Wagnalls, 1905), 12 volumes.

EncJud, *Encyclopaedia Judaica* (Jerusalem: Keter, 1971), 16 volumes.

Str-B, *Kommentar zum Neuen Testament aus Talmud und Midrasch*, by (H. Strack and) P. Billerbeck (Munich: Beck, 1924–1961), 6 volumes.

Strack and Stemberger, *Introduction to the Talmud and Midrash*, by H. Strack and G. Stemberger (Minneapolis: Fortress, 1992).

LSJ, *A Greek-English Lexicon*, by H. Liddell, R. Scott and H. Jones (Oxford: Clarendon, 1966⁹).

BAGD, *A Greek-English Lexicon of the New Testament and Other Early Christian Literature*, by W. Bauer, W. Arndt, F. Gingrich and F. Danker (Chicago: University of Chicago, 1979²).

*Chambers Murray, latin-english Dictionary*, ed. W. Smith and J. Lockwood (Edinburgh: Chambers; London: Murray, 1986).

IDB, *The Interpreter's Dictionary of the Bible*, ed. G. Buttrick et al. (New York and Nashville: Abingdon Press, 1962), four volumes. Supplementary Volume, ed. K. Crim, 1976.

RGG⁴, *Religion in Geschichte und Gegenwart*, ed. Hans Dieter Betz et al. (Tübingen: Mohr Siebeck, 1998–).

TRE, *Theologische Realenzyklopädie*, ed. Gerhard Krause and Gerhard Müller (Berlin: de Gruyter, 1977–2002), 34 volumes.

# About the Author

Roger David Aus, b. 1940, studied English and German at St. Olaf College, and theology at Harvard Divinity School, Luther Theological Seminary, and Yale University, from which he received the Ph.D. degree in New Testament Studies in 1971. He is an ordained clergyman of the Evangelical Lutheran Church in America and pastor emeritus of the German-speaking Luthergemeinde in Berlin-Reinickendorf, Germany.

## Other volumes by Roger David Aus

*My Name Is "Legion."* Palestinian Judaic Traditions in Mark 5:1–20 and Other Gospel Texts (Studies in Judaism; Lanham, MD: University Press of America, 2003). Including essays on Luke 4:16–30; Judas "Iscariot"; Luke 19:41–44; John 8:56–58; Matt 24:28 // Luke 17:37b; and Luke 13:34b // Matt 23:37b.

*The Stilling of the Storm.* Studies in Early Palestinian Judaic Traditions (International Studies in Formative Christianity and Judaism; Binghamton, NY: Global Publications, Binghamton University, 2000). Essays on Mark 4:35–41; 1:16–20; and Luke 24:13–35.

*"Caught in the Act," Walking on the Sea, and the Release of Barabbas Revisited* (South Florida Studies in the History of Judaism, 157; Atlanta: Scholars Press, 1998). Essays on John 7:53–8:11; Mark 6:45–52 par.; and 15:6–15 par.

*The Wicked Tenants and Gethsemane* (International Studies in Formative Christianity and Judaism, University of South Florida, 4; Atlanta: Scholars Press, 1996). Essays on Mark 12:1–9 par.; 14:32–42 par.; 2 Cor 12:1–10; and Judas' handing Jesus over to certain death through a kiss.

*Samuel, Saul and Jesus.* Three Early Palestinian Jewish Christian Gospel Haggadoth (South Florida Studies in the History of Judaism, 105; Atlanta: Scholars Press, 1994). Essays on Luke 2:41–51a; Mark 6:1–6a par.; and the prodigia at Jesus' crucifixion.

*Barabbas and Esther and Other Studies in the Judaic Illumination of Earliest Christianity* (South Florida Studies in the History of Judaism, 54; Atlanta: Scholars Press, 1992). Essays on Mark 15:6–15 par.; John 11:45–54; Luke 15:11–32; Matt 2:1–12; Gal 2:9; Isa 66:7, Revelation 12 and 2 Thessalonians 1; 2 Thess 2:6–7; Rom 11:25; and 2 Thess 1:3.

*Weihnachtsgeschichte, Barmherziger Samariter, Verlorener Sohn.* Studien zu ihrem jüdischen Hintergrund (ANTZ 2; Berlin: Institut Kirche und Judentum, 1988). Essays on Luke 2:1–20; 10:30–37; and 15:11–32.

*Water into Wine and the Beheading of John the Baptist.* Early Jewish-Christian Interpretation of Esther 1 in John 2:1–11 and Mark 6:17–29 (Brown Judaic Studies, 150; Atlanta: Scholars Press, 1988).

# Index of Modern Authors

Jacob Neusner

*The Aggadic Role in Halakhic Discourses.* Lanham. February 2001. University Press of America. Academic Studies in Ancient Judaism series. Volume I

*The Aggadic Role in Halakhic Discourses.* Lanham. February 2001. University Press of America. Academic Studies in Ancient Judaism series. Volume II

*The Aggadic Role in Halakhic Discourses.* Lanham. February 2001. University Press of America. Academic Studies in Ancient Judaism series. Volume III

*A Theological Commentary to the Midrash.* Lanham. April 2001. University Press of America. Academic Studies in Ancient Judaism series. Volume I. *Pesiqta deRab Kahana.*

*A Theological Commentary to the Midrash.* Lanham. March 2001. University Press of America. Academic Studies in Ancient Judaism series. - Volume II. *Genesis Raba.*

*A Theological Commentary to the Midrash.* Lanham. April 2001. University Press of America. Academic Studies in Ancient Judaism series. Volume III. *Song of Songs Rabbah*

*A Theological Commentary to the Midrash.* Lanham. April 2001. University Press of America. Academic Studies in Ancient Judaism series. Volume IV. *Leviticus Rabbah*

A Theological Commentary to the Midrash. Lanham. June 2001. University Press of America. Academic Studies in Ancient Judaism series. Volume V *Lamentations Rabbati*

*A Theological Commentary to the Midrash.* June 2001. University Press of America. Academic Studies in Ancient Judaism series. Volume VI. *Ruth Rabbah and Esther Rabbah I*

*A Theological Commentary to the Midrash.* June 2001. University Press of America. Academic Studies in Ancient Judaism series. Volume VII. *Sifra*

A Theological Commentary to the Midrash. July 2001. University Press of America. Academic Studies in Ancient Judaism series. Volume VIII. *Sifré to Numbers and Sifré to Deuteronomy*

A Theological Commentary to the Midrash. August 2001. University Press of America. Academic Studies in Ancient Judaism series.Volume IX. *Mekhilta Attributed to Rabbi Ishmael*

*The Unity of Rabbinic Discourse.* January 2001. University Press of America. Academic Studies in Ancient Judaism series. Volume I: *Aggadah in the Halakhah*

*The Unity of Rabbinic Discourse.* February 2001. University Press of America. Academic Studies in Ancient Judaism series. Volume II: *Halakhah in the Aggadah*

*The Unity of Rabbinic Discourse.* February 2001. University Press of America. Academic Studies in Ancient Judaism series. Volume III: *Halakhah and Aggadah in Concert*